THE TICKET-SPLITTER

A New Force in American Politics

THE
TICKET-SPLITTER
A New Force in American Politics

by

WALTER DE VRIES
LANCE TARRANCE, JR.

Foreword by David S. Broder

WILLIAM B. EERDMANS PUBLISHING COMPANY
Grand Rapids, Michigan

Dedicated to
Lois De Vries
and
Gg Tarrance

Contents

Some Acknowledgments

The initial research and writing of this book were done by Walter De Vries during a travel study grant from the Ford Foundation in the first half of 1968, and then continued at the Institute of Politics, Harvard University, during the 1968-69 academic year. Richard E. Neustadt, Director of the Institute, generously awarded De Vries with the Institute fellowship, which encouraged him to continue his writing, and Kathy Fowler gave her editing and typing skills to the manuscript.

While this work was progressing, Lance Tarrance was conducting parallel work on the ticket-splitter concept with data from Texas and national official election statistics, confirming many of the results De Vries had gotten in Michigan.

The entire ticket-splitter concept, however, might not have been developed and tested, had not former Michigan Governor George Romney—now Secretary of the Department of Housing and Urban Development—supported the research on Michigan ticket-splitters during the years 1962 through 1966. Governor Romney also supported research on national ticket-splitters during 1967-68, and was one of the first to recognize the need for post-election studies.

Governor William Milliken of Michigan continued the support of basic research on the ticket-splitters, broadening the research to include studies of their use of the various media and also supporting a good deal of experimental work in telephoning and the measurement of the effectiveness of campaign techniques.

Throughout the 1960's De Vries worked closely with Fredrick Currier, President of Market Opinion Research of

Detroit. Currier, before all other professional pollsters, saw the futility of trying to adapt the then most accepted theories of voting behavior to campaign strategy. His thinking was critical to our examination of the ticket-splitter, and his skills were at work in almost all of the polling research conducted for Governors Romney and Milliken.

Others who have helped us think through these problems or have edited parts of this book are Robert Colonna of Politicon, Inc.; Richard Fleming, former Associate Research Director of the Republican National Committee; Edward Nichols of Ed Nichols Associates; Richard Schweitzer, former Research Director for the Washington State Republican Committee; Dr. Richard Smolka of American University; and Robert Squier, President of The Communications Company in Washington, D.C.

The first drafts of the manuscript produced in early 1971 were typed diligently by Mrs. Sallie Ruffo. Miss Katy Martin combined her editing expertise with her typing skills to produce the final draft.

We thank them all.

Walter De Vries
Lance Tarrance, Jr.

Ann Arbor, Michigan

Foreword

Considering the time, energy and effort that go into the discussion of politics in this country, it is remarkable how poorly we understand what takes place in our elections. For the last decade and a half I have made my living reporting American politics, and I am prepared to say that I believe myself to be as dissatisified as Vice President Spiro Agnew with the output of my fellow journalists and myself. Further, at the risk of offending my academic friends, I would add, in candor, that I do not gain great enlightenment from what they write about the dynamics of democratic decision-making, either.

This discontent is shared by the public, and I think with good reason. We write repetitiously and at great length about what takes place in our elections, but what do we tell them that is of real use? Very little, I fear.

Consider, for example, our coverage of candidates. We focus on their personalities, their charisma or lack thereof, their oratorical and leadership styles, their use of staff, their capacities as organizers, administrators, fund-raisers and salesmen. Secondarily, we catalogue their positions on the issues and try, by our often-dim lights, to judge their "statesmanship" quotient or the degree of political prudence they display. In recent years, some of my more sophisticated colleagues have tried to explain to their readers the techniques of the "new politics"—polling, electronic data process, advertising and the rest of the fresh tricks in the campaign bag.

But the judgments we have made about candidates do not stand up very well under scrutiny. To cite only one of many examples, I think that most journalists involved in the coverage of the 1964 campaign now feel a certain chagrin about the stereotypes they helped create that year. Lyndon B. Johnson was depicted as a forceful but prudent leader, firmly dedicated to peace in Vietnam and the building of a "Great Society" at home, while Barry Goldwater was drawn as a belligerent, temperamentally unbalanced right-wing extremist of dubious intellect and warlike demeanor. Those caricatures are on our conscience.

If we have been—as I would argue—too often inaccurate in our depiction of candidates' personalities and positions, we have done not much better in describing their campaign techniques. Frankly, as those techniques have become more esoteric and covert than we are accustomed to seeing employed, we are more often out of our depth. You can count on the fingers of your hands the number of reporters who *really* understand opinion survey research, or the use of computers in political campaigns. As Joe McGinniss demonstrated in *The Selling of the President*, it is ridiculously easy to gull us with a modern media campaign—and indeed to maneuver us into playing our predetermined role in carrying out the candidate's media strategy.

We also write a great deal about the political parties— their leadership struggles, the state of their financial and organizational health, their efforts to reform themselves and to define their positions on the issues. We have covered meetings of the national committees, the state chairmen, the policy councils and the reform commissions and have probably told our readers more about the internal party struggles than most of them care to know.

Our concentration on the political parties seems increasingly irrelevant, as the evidence mounts that very little in American politics can be explained in party terms. The Senate for years has been controlled by *ad hoc* coalitions, formed on particular issues with a blithe disregard for the center aisle. The House is increasingly coming to behave the same way. For half the time I have worked in Washington, we have had a President of one party and a Congress of the other; what relevance, then, has the idea of party responsibility?

It is clear that party affiliation is a fragile basis for

attempting to explain the mood or predict the behavior of the voters. The Gallup and Harris polls and the surveys of the University of Michigan Center for Political Studies all show that independents are growing in numbers at the expense of both parties, rivaling the Republicans in size and creeping up on the Democrats. In the last Presidential election, we had a major third-party movement and there is prospect for 1972 of a fourth-party movement on the left as well. When over half the voters now split their tickets and millions of Americans say, with great pride, that they vote for the man, not the party, it behooves us to shift our attention to the voters—and particularly to those "independents" who seem increasingly to be the target of the candidates and the determiners of the election outcome.

We don't know much about them. They turn up in the polls and we meet them when we do our own door-knocking surveys at campaign time, but neither we nor the academics seem to know much about the ticket-splitters and what makes them tick.

Those of us who have come out of political science departments in the last dozen years have as our bible, of course, *The American Voter*, the classic study by the University of Michigan scholars. But rich as it is in data and insights on other aspects of voting behavior, it has not been very helpful to us on this particular question.

For one thing, its description of the independent voter is more than a little disquieting to the notions of democracy we carry in our heads, and, more directly, to our professional pride. We like to think that a free press—and the information on politics it purveys—plays a crucial role in determining the choice of our leaders and the public policies they pursue. But the independents, as depicted in *The American Voter*, are people who "tend as a group to be somewhat less involved . . . have somewhat poorer knowledge of the issues, their image of the candidates is fainter, their interest in the campaign is less, their concern over the outcome is relatively slight, and their choice between competing candidates . . . seems much less to spring from discovered evaluations of the elements of national politics."

This is, as I say, disquieting to our notions of democracy

and of our own role in the political system. Moreover, it makes us doubt that the candidates know what they are doing, because most of the activity we can see in a campaign is designed to activate and reach those independents.

This book offers quite a different view of this crucial and growing body of voters. At root, the difference between the independents of *The American Voter* and the ticket-splitters De Vries and Tarrance describe in this volume is a difference of concept.

The concept of independents used in the University of Michigan study (and also in Gallup's and Harris's polls) is based on self-perception and self-description. They are voters who *call* themselves independents rather than Democrats or Republicans. On the other hand, the concept of ticket-splitters used in this book is based on the voters' *behavior*, being defined as those who move back and forth across the ballot rather than voting exclusively for candidates of a single party.

The two are not identical. These authors say that less than half the behavioral ticket-splitters are self-described independents. Dr. Gallup's post-1968 study found that 45 percent of the self-described Republicans and 47 percent of the self-described Democrats actually said they voted a split ticket, while 25 percent of the independents said they voted a straight ticket.

At the level of debate between two concepts, I have no qualifications to judge the argument—if there is one—between De Vries and Tarrance and the social psychologists who teach political science. My hope is that if this book raises as serious an intellectual challenge to the classification scheme of *The American Voter* as it appears to a layman to do, we will be allowed to watch the debate among the scholars and to gain instruction from it. What I can say, as one involved in reporting and analyzing politics for the public, is that I find this scheme helpful in understanding things that have been very puzzling to explain.

For one thing, it gives me a picture of the ticket-splitter that is closer to the kind of voter I picture as determining the outcome of close races. "The ticket-splitter," De Vries and Tarrance write, "is slightly younger, somewhat more educated, somewhat more white-collar, and more suburban than the typical middle-class voter. In addition, the ticket-splitter tends to consume more media output about politics and is more active politically than the straight Democrat (but less than the straight Republican)."

In Michigan, they found the profiles of the independents and the ticket-splitters quite at variance. The self-described independent tended to be a woman of 50-59, a Protestant, and the wife of a relatively low-income union member-skilled worker. The typical ticket-splitter, on the other hand, was a Catholic male between thirty and forty-nine, who managed or owned a business and was in the middle-income bracket.

Second, their description accords somewhat more comfortably with my notions of what the idealized democratic voter is like and also helps me understand the rationality of much of contemporary campaign strategy.

The ticket-splitter, they say, bases his decision on his judgment of the candidate's ability, personality, his competence to handle the job and his stands on the issues. Party identification is relatively unimportant to him.

He gets the information on which he bases his judgments primarily from television (ah, well!), particularly television news shows, documentaries and discussion programs, and secondarily from newspaper editorials and family talks. Advertising—even the much-vaunted TV spots—rank well down on his list of influential factors.

"The ticket-splitter," they say, "did not emerge from our data as a one-issue person or as a voter who could be easily reached by highly emotional appeals. Rather he emerged as a *complex* voter who had a ready grasp and knowledge of the campaign issues and who was oriented toward problem-solving by candidates rather than by political parties."

Having described him, the authors then tell how this knowledge can be used to shape a campaign strategy, giving great detail on the gubernatorial campaign in Michigan in 1970, which was certainly one of the most clearly "managed" campaigns I have ever covered.

At this point, it is quite tempting to say, "Well, dandy." We now know who is deciding our elections, and how they make up their minds, and how to influence their decisions, and now we can go forward into the 70's, when the wave of new young voters, who carry their party allegiance even more lightly than do their parents, will make this truly the era of the ticket-splitter.

But that is not satisfactory—at least to me—either at the intellectual level or at the level of democratic values.

It seems to me that these authors have given our understanding of voting behavior a great boost forward, but that their insights are the occasion for further research, not for shutting off the subject. I would like to know what explains the diminution of straight-ticket voting and the general reduction in the saliency of party identification as an organizing principle for electoral action. Is it a product of affluence and increasing education? Does it reflect a blurring of the strongly felt issues of the American past? Is it a product of the television and computer revolutions? Is it now chic to split your ticket? What is at the root of this phenomenon?

I ask those questions because I am not at all certain in my own mind that the development of independent voting habits—or ticket-splitting, whichever term you prefer—is automatically the boon to our politics and government that many people suppose it to be. As these authors note, the period of the 1960's, which saw such an upsurge in ticket-splitting, also saw a decline in voting participation and unmistakable evidence of growing public disillusionment with politics and government as such.

The 1960's also saw (and unfortunately, the 1970's have continued) a pattern of divided government, at both the national and state level, that in my judgment has contributed directly to the frustration we all feel in reaching our national objectives. In short, I think it needs to be considered whether ticket-splitting is a costly political habit— costly in terms of the effect it has on the capacity of government to resolve those issues which aggravate and frustrate our people.

De Vries and Tarrance suggest in their concluding pages that the techniques of modern political campaigning be applied to government; specifically, that public opinion be monitored constantly to give those in government a set of "political indicators" by which they can judge the acceptability of various courses of action.

That idea has merit. But equally, I would suggest, we need to improve our system of communicating to the voters a set of "governmental indicators," specifically, an understanding of the conditions that make it possible for government to be not only representative but effective. In my view, party responsibility is one—and perhaps the most important—of those conditions.

But that discussion is for another time and place. What all can agree on is that the people who are crucial in determining our political future, whether it be one of frustration or of accomplishment, are the ticket-splitters. We literally cannot know too much about them for our own good. And this book is a good first step in understanding them.

—David S. Broder
National Political Correspondent,
Washington Post

CHAPTER 1

Recent Voting Behavior
and the Independents

We will never have a time again, in my opinion, in this country when you are going to have a polarization of only Democrats versus Republicans. . . . I think you are going to have the Independents *controlling basically the balance of power.*

President Richard M. Nixon
ABC Television and Radio Interview
March 22, 1971

No analyst of American politics could have predicted with any certainty the voting behavior of the American electorate during the 1960's. Who could have foreseen that:

split outcomes in gubernatorial and U. S. Senatorial elections in individual states would soar to more than 50% of those contests in the five biennial elections from 1960 to 1970;

the number of Congressional districts with split outcomes (between Presidential and Congressional candidates of the same party) would rise to 33.3% of the 435 House seats in 1964 and then remain at a high 31.6% in the 1968 election;

in 1968, split outcomes would occur in 55% of the 20 states with elections below the office of governor (lieutenant governor, secretary of state, attorney general, treasurer, auditor, or controller);

George Wallace would gain a place for himself in the American Independent Party on the ballot in all fifty states, and then go on to win nearly 10 million votes in the 1968 Presidential election;

in 1968, the American voters would put a newly elected President of one party, with a Congress controlled in both houses by the opposition party, at the head of the first divided national government since 1848;

in 1969, with 42% of the voters identifying themselves as Democrats and only 28% as Republicans (30% as independents), Republican governors would control eight of the ten largest states, and, in total, Republican governors would be in office in states where 70% of the national population live; and,

in 1969, twenty of the states would have governors of one party, with one or more houses of the state legislature controlled by the other political party?

Or, to place these voting patterns of the 1960's in terms of their impact on political personalities, who could have predicted that:

in 1964, President Lyndon B. Johnson would take Michigan with 66.8% of the vote while Republican George Romney would win 56.1% of the vote for governor—from the same electorate;

in 1966, Republican John Tower would receive a plurality of 198,600 votes in the U. S. Senate race while Democratic governor John Connally amassed a plurality of 669,500 votes; and,

in the 1960 Arkansas election, third-party candidate George Wallace would win the Presidential contest while Republican Winthrop Rockefeller would be re-elected governor and Democrat J. William Fulbright returned to the U. S. Senate?

Indeed, how could anyone have predicted that in 1970 the state electorates would:

elect Republican Ronald Reagan as governor and Democrat John Tunney as U. S. Senator in California;

elect Democrat John Gilligan as governor and Republican Robert Taft as U. S. Senator in Ohio; and,

in Pennsylvania, elect Democrat Milton Shapp as governor while re-electing Republican Hugh Scott to the U. S. Senate.

Examples of ticket-splitting during the 1960's are plentiful. Clearly, some fundamental changes in American voting behavior occurred during the 1960's, more than in any other decade since the depression years of the 1930's.

Some observers have seen these changes in the 1960's as a major realignment of the two political parties. Others have thought they detected the emergence of new coalitions of voters or the building of new majorities. In fact, some analysts believe that we are experiencing the disintegration of the two-party system as we have known it, arguing that if this trend continues, the Republican and Democratic parties may be completely removed as the major variables in most elections. A few analysts now believe that rather than party, the issues, the candidates' views, and the use of the media both by the candidates and by the voters are now the most important factors in a voter's decision.

Whatever the explanation, we do know that something happened to American voters during the politically turbulent years from 1960 to 1970. Those years produced a whole set of political paradoxes which have yet to be explained. And that is what this book is all about—to articulate a new and more plausible explanation for what happened to the American voters during those years.

When large numbers of voters began to split their tickets between the candidates of the Republican and Democratic parties, not only did their personal politics change, but these voters began a process that would have enormous consequences for all governments across the nation. This book is about that new force at work in America. We will try to understand this new "independent" voter and to what extent he differs from the traditional independent described in much of the research and writings of political scientists and other analysts. We will examine the way the ticket-splitter makes up his mind about politics and government. Then we shall try to demonstrate how this knowledge about the ticket-splitter can be applied to campaign strategies. The book concludes with some speculation as to what the ticket-splitter and the campaigns of the 1970's may be like.

TRENDS

Throughout American history, most voters were straight-ticket voters, and until World War II more than 80% were still so classified. Through the 1950's, this statistic remained around 60-70%. The Survey Research Center found that 66% of those voting in the Presidential race in 1952 voted a straight ticket; in 1956 the percentage dropped to 61%. However, in his 1968 post-election study, George Gallup found that only 43% of the American voters said they had voted a straight party ticket. This identified a sudden shift in voting behavior; more than half of those voting said they had split their ticket.[1]

Political journalist Bruce Biossat described the case for diminishing partisanship in this way:

> ... a notable, demonstrable phenomenon is that splitting is growing all the time.... Where once a fair proportion of voters might vote for one party's presidential nominee but then go "regular" through the rest of the slate, now millions are picking and choosing carefully among the various party candidates for a sizable range of state offices.... Scholars are inclined to judge the splitting phenomenon as an unmistakable mark of an enlarging political sophistication of the electorate. The knowledge explosion, fueled mightily by television, lays bare to the American citizens the nature of men and issues as never before. Thus, voters have become inevitably more selective.[2]

[1] Gallup Post-election Survey, December 1968.
[2] "Ticket Splitter—Selective Voter," *Washington Daily News*, March 31, 1970.

The decrease in straight party voting in the late 1960's is associated with the weakening of old-line party organizations and special-interest group leaders. Except for Mayor Daley—a political anachronism—the urban political machine of the first half of the twentieth century has almost disappeared; so have the people who acted as intermediaries or brokers for party members at state and national levels. The decline in the brokerage power of political organization leaders, of professional, business, and labor groups, of educational groups, and even of strong religious and ethnic organizations reflects the spread of voter independence and estrangement from strong organizational ties and bloc-vote commitments.

Another important shift has taken place in the way American voters psychologically identify themselves. At one point in 1969, Gallup found that more people considered themselves independents than Republicans (30% to 28%). Much of this shift in identification has occurred since 1966. Prior to that time, self-identified independents constituted only about 20% of the electorate. Today the younger the age group, the larger the number who identify as independents. Between the ages of twenty-one and twenty-nine years, 42% identify as independents. On Northern urban campuses, more than 50% of the students identify themselves as independents. Even though increasing age tends to correspond with increasing partisanship, the statistical base of young self-identified independents is disproportionately large today.

CAN PARTY IDENTIFICATION EXPLAIN ELECTION OUTCOMES ANY MORE?

American voters not only perceive and identify themselves differently than they did several years ago, but they behave differently in the voting booth as well. We believe that the real test of the voter's independence is whether or not he splits his ticket. A voter may say he is an independent, but this can be confirmed only by his actual voting behavior. True independence is defined in this book as actual ticket-splitting, since this is what ultimately counts at the campaign level.

In the 1960's, private research by Walter De Vries suggested that ticket-splitters were coming mainly from the ranks of the Republican Party. Now it appears that the split-ticket trend has shifted to include many previously straight Democratic Party adherents as well. The Democratic Party will not likely be able to hold all of those who now identify with it—currently about 45% of the electorate.

For many elections, core Republican Party strength has been smaller than that of the Democratic Party. *The American Voter* and subsequent studies by the University of Michigan's Center for Political Studies have repeatedly documented this fact. For example, among self-identified strong and weak Republicans, the University of Michigan has established these ominous statistics for Republicans, indicating that their party has stabilized into a permanent minority party while the number of self-identified independents has steadily increased:

PERCEIVED PARTY IDENTIFICATION
UNIVERSITY OF MICHIGAN[3]

	Oct. 1952	Oct. 1956	Oct. 1960	Nov. 1962	Oct. 1964	Nov. 1966	Nov. 1968	Nov. 1970	Trend 1952-1970
Strong/Weak Republicans	27	29	27	28	24	25	24	25	-2
Strong/Weak Democrats	47	44	46	46	51	45	45	43	-4
All Independents	22	24	23	22	23	28	30	31	+9
Don't know	4	3	4	4	2	2	1	1	-3

Gallup and Harris polls over the last decade have presented the same picture:

[3] See Appendix H for the complete set of data by the University of Michigan.

SELF-ADMINISTERED MEASUREMENT OF PARTISANSHIP
BY GEORGE GALLUP POLLS

	1960	1962	1964	1966	1967	1968	1969	1970	1971	Trend 1960-1971
Republican	30	29	25	27	27	27	28	29	28	−2
Democrat	47	48	53	48	44	46	42	45	45	−2
Independent	23	23	22	25	29	27	30	26	27	+4

SELF-ADMINISTERED MEASUREMENT OF PARTISANSHIP
BY HARRIS POLLS

	1965	1970	1971	Trend 1965-1971
Republican	31	33	30	−1
Democrat	52	48	47	−5
Independent	17	19	23	+6

Yet the Republicans have remained highly competitive during the last two decades—in Presidential and lately in U. S. Senatorial and gubernatorial races. The Republican Party has won three of the last five Presidential elections in this country and has increased its share in the U. S. Senate at the expense of the Democratic Party by a net increase of ten U. S. Senators since 1960. At one time in the last decade (1969), Republican state governors controlled eight of the ten largest states as well as almost 70% of the national population.

How have Republican candidates been able to win during the last two decades when measurements of party attachments show the G. O. P. at almost a two-to-one disadvantage? We suggest that Republicans have been capturing a heavy majority of independent voters, including self-perceived independents, as well as holding the vast percentage of the Republican electorate.

Using the biennial U. S. House races shown in Table 1 as another competitive party measure, we see that Republicans appear to have a nationwide Congressional strength (even when the Southern states are included) in the range of 45 to 50%, depending on the election year.[4] These major party U. S. House statistics for Republicans are nearly double the traditional self-identity figures used by the University of Michigan (i.e., only about 25% for those who identify themselves as Republicans).[5]

TABLE 1

Geopolitical Regions (States)	1966 Rep. House Vote %	1968 Rep. House Vote %	1970-71 Rep. House Vote %
New England (6)	43.5	50.1	45.6
Middle Atlantic (4)	49.8	49.6	46.8
E. Middle West (5)	54.2	54.6	49.9
W. Middle West (7)	54.2	52.9	49.1
South (10)	32.3	34.1	33.5
Border (5)	47.1	46.7	42.1
Mountain (8)	52.2	54.8	50.1
Pacific (5)	52.1	52.5	47.5
Total:	48.7	48.9	45.8

Assuming that all "strong" and "weak" Republican partisans and all Republican-leaning independents voted straight Republican, there is still a discrepancy between the self-classified measurement of the University of Michigan Center for Political Studies and the political realities of Republican election victories:

[4] *Elections 1970, A Summary Report,* published by the Republican National Committee, March 1971.

[5] *Ibid.*

1970[6]	%
Strong Republicans	15
Weak Republicans	10
Independents-leaning Republican	8
	33% . . . . . 17% + unaccounted for?

Because Republicans must depend so heavily on non-Republican votes, their campaigns for the Presidency and statewide offices have been and will continue to be much more sophisticated than those of Democratic Party candidates.

Since World War II American voters might assume that it is a natural condition to have a President of one party and a Congress of the other. Moreover, during the last decade, this phenomenon has been extended to state governments so that ticket-splitting is occurring not only at the national but also at the state level.[7]

There are very few "safe" statewide offices left outside of the South. Governors of many states are confronted with hostile legislatures that are controlled by those of another partisan stripe. Ticket-splitters are reducing the number of one-party states not only for New England Republicans, but also for Southern Democrats, and are increasing the number of competitive—closely won or lost—races all over the nation. Some examples of heavy ticket-splitting in the recent elections of 1970 are presented below:

[6] Appendix H.

[7] After the 1970 elections, 21 states had incongruent political party situations: Republican governor and Democrat legislature (7), Republican governor and split-control legislature (4), Democrat governor and Republican legislature (6), and Democrat governor and split-control legislature (4).

	Voting	
	Republican	Democrat
Maryland		
U.S. Senate	485,000	460,000
Governor	314,000	640,000
T-S difference	+171,000	−180,000
Arizona		
U.S. Senate	228,000	180,000
Governor	210,000	202,000
T-S difference	+18,000	−22,000
California		
U.S. Senate	2,878,000	3,497,000
Governor	3,440,000	2,939,000
T-S difference	−562,000	+558,000
Ohio		
U.S. Senate	1,566,000	1,495,000
Governor	1,383,000	1,726,000
T-S difference	+183,000	−231,000
Pennsylvania		
U.S. Senate	1,874,000	1,654,000
Governor	1,543,000	2,043,000
T-S difference	+331,000	−389,000

Ticket-splitting is not an isolated or regional phenomenon; it is widespread—a political fact of life in today's election campaigns.

THE PRESIDENT AND THE CONGRESS

If ballot-splitting should continue through the Sixties it will soon be "un-American" for President and Congress to belong to the same party.[8]

[8] Richard E. Neustadt, *Presidential Power, The Politics of Leadership* (New York: Wiley, 1961), p. 189.

Richard E. Neustadt need have no fear that the executive and legislative branches of our government are in any danger of becoming "un-American." Over the last forty years, even when Republicans have won the White House, the Democrats have controlled the Congress by heavy majorities.[9] In 1968 we returned to the familiar course of events by electing a Republican President along with a heavily Democratic Senate and House of Representatives.

Political scientists have traditionally defined ticket-splitting as the difference between the vote for candidates for President and the U. S. House of Representatives.[10] Milton Cummings, in an article on ticket-splitting that dealt primarily with voters who split their tickets in the 1956 and 1964 Presidential and Congressional elections, detected that on the average there has been more ticket-splitting since World War II than before.[11]

While the 1956 and 1964 Presidential elections may be considered ticket-splitter rampages, the data shows that those elections are not far from the general trend of increased ticket-splitting between the 1956 and 1968 elections.

[9] The Republicans have not had complete control of both the executive and legislative branches for nearly 40 years except for the brief period of 1952 to 1954.

[10] A good example of this is in *Voting in Postwar Federal Elections* by Edward F. Cox (Wright State University, Dayton, Ohio, 1968). The author constructed a measurement of minimal split-ticket voting in Federal elections by a comparison of party-vote changes in Presidential and Congressional contests. In only the Presidential-year elections during the last 30 years or so, Cox calculated the following figures which represented the minimum net percentages of voters in each respective election who switched parties while voting in any two Federal contests and revealed the considerably higher trend of splitting in postwar years than in those earlier: 1932—3.19; 1936—3.82; 1940—3.16; 1944—2.96; 1948—5.35; 1952—6.37; 1956—6.80; 1960—5.22; 1964—7.24.

[11] "Split-Ticket Voting and the Presidency and Congress," in *Congressmen and the Electorate: Elections for the U.S. House and the President, 1920-1964*, ed. Milton Cummings, Jr. (New York: Free Press, 1967), p. 46.

TABLE 2

CONGRESSIONAL DISTRICTS WITH SPLIT ELECTION
RESULTS: DISTRICTS CARRIED BY A PRESIDENTIAL
NOMINEE AND A U.S. HOUSE NOMINEE OF DIFFERENT
PARTIES, 1920-1968[12]

Year & Party of Winning Presidential Candidate	Number of Districts	Number of Districts With Split Results	Percent Split Election Results
1920 R	344	11	3.2
1924 R	356	42	11.8
1928 R	359	68	18.9
1932 D	355	50	14.1
1936 D	361	51	14.1
1940 D	362	53	14.6
1944 D	367	41	11.2
1948 D	422	90	21.3
1952 R	435	84	19.3
1956 R	435	130	29.9
1960 D	437	114	26.1
1964 D	435	145	33.3
1968 R[13]	435	139	31.6

STATEWIDE ELECTIONS

Statewide patterns of voting over the years also evidence the trend toward increased ticket-splitting. Split outcomes in state gubernatorial and U. S. Senate elections averaged only 18% during the election period of 1932 to 1950 (ten biennial elections), but in the 1952 to 1960 election period (five biennial elections) it was 21%, and since 1960 it has been 52% (five biennial elections)!

In the past thirty years, there has been a higher percentage of split outcomes during Presidential-year elections

[12] The data for the years 1924-1964 is from the Milton Cummings, Jr., article cited in the previous footnote.

[13] For those who keep records of this sort, the 1968 vote in the Presidential and Congressional elections breaks down by Congressional districts as follows: Humphrey and Democratic winner, 31%; Nixon and Republican winner, 37%; Humphrey and Republican winner, 6%; Nixon and Democratic winner, 14%; Wallace and Democratic winner, 11%; and Wallace and Republican winner, 1%.

TABLE 3

SPLIT OUTCOMES IN GUBERNATORIAL AND U.S. SENATORIAL ELECTIONS: 1914-1970[14]

Year	States with Simultaneous Elections	Number of Split Outcomes	Percent: Split[15] Outcomes
1914	22	6	27.3
1916	24	5	20.8
1918	22	1	4.5
1920	24	0	0.0
1922	22	5	22.7
1924	26	1	3.8
1926	24	4	16.7
1928	24	4	16.7
1930	24	5	20.8
1932	23	3	13.0
1934	22	3	13.6
1936	24	2	8.3
1938	24	4	16.7
1940	26	11	42.3
1942	23	3	13.0
1944	22	6	27.3
1946	24	1	4.2
1948	22	4	18.2
1950	24	5	20.8
1952	22	6	27.3
1954	25	6	24.0
1956	20	3	15.0
1958	22	4	18.2
1960	19	5	36.3
1962	27	12	44.4
1964	18	10	55.6
1966	22	13	59.1
1968	15	9	60.0
1970	24	11	45.8

[14] From an unpublished paper by Howard Reiter, Harvard University, John Fitzgerald Kennedy School of Government, March 1969.

[15] Reiter noted in his paper that a closer measure of ticket-splitting would be the difference in the party breakdown of the vote. For

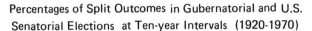

Percentages of Split Outcomes in Gubernatorial and U.S. Senatorial Elections at Ten-year Intervals (1920-1970)

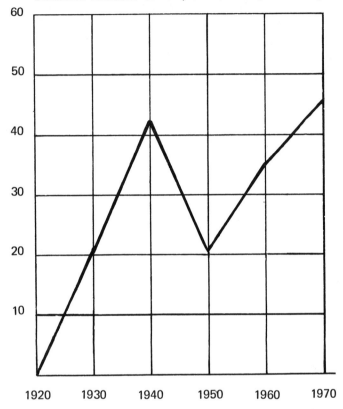

than the off years. There is little doubt that since 1940 there has been a steady increase in the amount of ticket-splitting in statewide contests involving the governor and U. S. Senator (see Table 3 and the accompanying chart).

In the 1970 state elections in states with both U. S. Senate and gubernatorial contests, the ticket-splitting pat-

example, if the Republican nominee for governor received 40% of the vote and the Republican nominee for senator received 70% in the same election, it is probable that more voters split their tickets than if the percentages were 40% and 45%.

tern was not as strong as in the three previous elections. This might be partially explained by the switch in national administrations in 1968, or by mathematical chance, since in the apparently congruent elections in Maine, Arizona, and Rhode Island, the races for governor were almost "too close to call."

The 1968 election also saw twenty states with elections below the office of governor—lieutenant governor, secretary of state, attorney general, treasurer, and auditor or controller—in which eleven states (55%) split control between the two major parties. Twenty-eight of the fifty states (56%) had statewide election officials of both political parties in 1969.

TABLE 4

1970 ELECTION RESULTS

Congruent Party Patterns			Incongruent Party Patterns		
	Sen.	Gov.		Sen.	Gov.
Arizona	R	R	Alaska	R	D
Connecticut	R	R	California	D	R
Florida	D	D	Hawaii	R	D
Maine	D	D	Maryland	R	D
Minnesota	D	D	Massachusetts	D	R
Missouri	D	D	Michigan	D	R
Nevada	D	D	Nebraska	R	D
New Mexico	D	D	New York	C	R
Rhode Island	D	D	Ohio	R	D
Tennessee	R	R	Pennsylvania	R	D
Texas	D	D	Wyoming	D	R
Vermont	R	R			
Wisconsin	D	D			
Total: 13			Total: 11		

GOVERNORS AND STATE LEGISLATURES

Ticket-splitting has also occurred between governors and state legislatures. After the 1968 Presidential elections, the

Republicans held the governorship and controlled both houses of the legislature in fifteen states, and the Democrats controlled the governorship and legislature in thirteen states, making a total of twenty-eight one-party-controlled states. In 1971 the number dropped by one to twenty-seven.

TABLE 5

CONTROL OF STATE GOVERNMENTS BY PARTY,
1969 & 1971
(Governor and State Legislature)

	No. of States 1969	No. of States 1971
Republican governor & Republican legislature	15	10
Republican governor & Non-partisan legislature	2	0
Republican governor & Split legislature	6	4
Republican governor & Democratic legislature	7	7
Democratic governor & Republican legislature	5	6
Democratic governor & Split legislature	2	2
Democratic governor & Democratic legislature	13	17

The split control of state government has increased from five in 1961 to nineteen in 1971. During that same ten-year period, the number of states in which Democrats controlled both houses decreased from twenty-nine to twenty-four.

MICHIGAN AND TEXAS—TWO EXAMPLES

Michigan is one of those states in which splitting the ballot in elections is rather difficult. All areas are equipped

with voting machines which let the voter pull one lever at
the top to vote a straight party ticket. If the voter wants to
split the ballot, he must move the lever for each office all
the way across the machine. It is sufficiently difficult to
split a ballot that some candidates have conducted vigor-
ous educational and propaganda programs on how to do
so. Whether they had any impact or not is difficult to
determine, but ticket-splitting in Michigan—as in all other
states—occurred at a phenomenal rate in 1964. President
Johnson (D) carried eighty of the eighty-three counties,
Governor George Romney (R) carried seventy-six, the
Republican candidate for attorney general carried twenty-
seven, and Barry Goldwater (R) carried three.

TICKET-SPLITTING IN MICHIGAN, 1964
PERCENT OF THE VOTE: STATEWIDE OFFICES[16]

Republican Ticket			Democratic Ticket		
	Vote %	Rep. % dif.		Vote %	Rep. % dif.
Governor: *Romney*[17]	56.1		President: *Johnson*	66.8	
Att'y. Gen.: Warshawsky	41.6	−14.5	U.S. Senate: *Hart*	64.5	−2.3
Sec'y. of State: Green	36.9	−19.2	Sec'y. of State: *Hare*	63.1	−3.7
U.S. Senator: Peterson	35.5	−20.6	Att'y. Gen.: *Kelley*	59.4	−7.4
President: Goldwater	33.2	−22.9	Governor: Staebler	43.9	−22.9

The subsequent elections of 1966 continued to feel the
pronounced effect of split-ticket voting.[18] For example,
look at the major statewide elections in Texas that year:

[16] From an unpublished paper by Glen L. Bachelder, "Michigan
Votes—1964: A 'Swinging' Election," Michigan State University,
December 17, 1964.

[17] Winners italicized.

[18] Nationwide in 1966 there were also over a hundred Congressional districts that elected a *Democratic* Congressman but at the
same time voted for a *Republican* senatorial or gubernatorial candidate. Regionally it broke down as follows: East 39, Midwest 13,
South 38, and West 23.

	Republican Votes	Democratic Votes
U.S. Senate	842,500—John G. Tower (R)	643,900
Governor	368,000	1,037,500—John B. Connally (D)
T-S difference	+474,500	−393,600

On the official ballot arrangement in Texas that year, U. S. Senator John Tower's position on the ballot was allegedly designed so that he was "hidden" among the other traditionally Democratic state election officials. Yet he was overwhelmingly victorious and was the only Republican in a Texas statewide contest to win that year.[19]

Official Ballot Order in 1966	Republican Candidates	Democratic Candidates	Results: Democratic Vote %
Governor	Kennerly	Connally	72.8%
Lt. Governor	Dibrell	Smith	71.2
U.S. Senate	Tower	Carr	43.1
Attorney General	Stewart	Martin	69.6
State Treasurer	Gilmer	James	70.9
Land Commissioner	Fay	Sadler	67.5

In summary, more work needs to be done on the effect ballot arrangement and the structure of the voting machine have on ticket-splitting. The evidence suggests, however, that these things do not have much relationship today to the voters' motivation and ability to split the ticket as was thought by some scholars.[20]

[19] See also *Texas Precinct Votes '66*, by Lance Tarrance, distributed by the Southern Methodist University Press, Dallas, Texas.

[20] See "The Effect of the Australian Ballot Reform on Split-ticket Voting 1876-1908," by Jerrold G. Rusk, *American Political Science Review*, December 1970 (a fascinating article on the importance of the ballot in American politics).

SUMMARY

Michigan will be a major focus of this book since much of the first research on ticket-splitting was conducted there. But the results of studies in Michigan are remarkably similar to the results found on a national level, and we will also refer to an extensive unpublished national study. This study describes the ticket-splitter as a new construct on the electoral scene. Unlike the "floating" voter, who changes his party preference between elections but does vote a straight ticket in any given election, and unlike the traditional independent, who refuses to be classified with either of the two major parties, the ticket-splitter is likely to be basically a Republican or Democrat, but one who occasionally splits off to vote for a candidate of another party. The ticket-splitter we have mainly in mind is one who splits between Presidential and gubernatorial candidates or who splits between gubernatorial candidates and candidates for lower statewide offices. More specifically, we have concentrated on Michigan voters who split their tickets between Republican candidates for governor and attorney general in four elections—1962, 1964, 1966, and 1970.

We do not claim that party identification no longer plays an important role in the American elective process, nor are we imagining the end of political parties. Our intention is to bring party identification into clearer focus by studying it under actual campaign situations. Although we do not consider the party affiliation of the candidates at the top of the ticket (President, governor, senator, representative) as any longer supremely important, we do think that party identification probably still plays a major role in voting behavior, particularly for races below the level of Congress.

In summary, this book will try to explain the impact ticket-splitters have had on the major statewide and national American political campaigns. It differs from most research studies in that it describes a new way to think about American voting behavior. It proposes ways in which these findings can be used in campaign strategies to reach this new kind of voter. Our findings are also intended to be suggestive and to invite further research into the split-ticket voter.

This book is meant to be neither a rigid technical document with correlation coefficients and multiple regressions nor a journalistic polemic with no hard data and consideration of campaign realities. It is intended to be a conceptualizing document about a new group of independent voters who, we believe, hold the balance of power in American politics.

CHAPTER 2

Independence in Voting–
A New Methodology

Unfortunately, up to now we have relied primarily on two limited criteria for measuring "independents": (1) Some objective measure through the use of official election statistics, such as a computation of split-ticket voting or of the fluctuation in party percentages; (2) some subjective measure, such as asking respondents in a survey whether they consider themselves to be partisans or "independents." Neither is satisfactory. The first is too narrow and rigid; the latter may not reveal who actually are the independents. For more reliable measures we need data on voting behavior, attitudes, and predispositions—self-perceptions may be completely erroneous.

Samuel Eldersveld, "The Independent
Vote," *American Political Science
Association Review*, September 1952

HISTORY AND IMPACT OF
DEFINITIONS OF "INDEPENDENCE"

Nearly everything written in the academic world about "independent voting" has been based on the self-administered definition: "Do you consider yourself an independent?" That, with some related concepts, has dominated voting behavior theory even though political reality has demanded a more precise measurement for many years.

The so-called independent voter was first discovered by political scientists around 1900. Since then, all the analyses of election statistics, all the aggregate studies and survey research have still failed to produce an understandable and relevant set of findings about independent voting behavior. Research on independent voting over the years by political scientists has been performed sporadically and without enthusiasm or thoroughness. As Samuel Eldersveld said in an article in 1952:

> Despite the use of unsatisfactory techniques and the generally unsystematic nature of our inquiries, many hunches, informative guesses, and even dogmatic generalizations have been articulated about the phenomenon of independent voting. . . . The truth is that the strategic significance of the "independents" has never been carefully studied, although we are quick to say that they hold the balance of power. . . .
>
> Independents may be many or few; they may be increasing or not; a real pattern may or may not exist; independents may be of many undetermined types; they may be intelligent or fickle; and the effects of independent voting on the political system may be beneficent or dangerous. The state of our knowledge about independent voting is obviously not precise, well documented, or unanimous.[1]

Eldersveld concluded:

> . . . until we systematically get at all the components of independence in voting through some objective measurement, we can never know with assurance the volume and direction of the tendency.[2]

It is regrettable that Eldersveld's advice was not heeded and that his concerns about the lack of data on voting independence were not met through more research. In short, the search for that "objective measurement" has not been productive.

The principal problem has always been one of definition. The earliest observers all meant to describe the same process or set of events, but because of the varied presuppositions they made, or because of the nature of their

[1] "The Independent Vote . . . ," *American Political Science Review*, September 1952, pp. 734-735.

[2] *Ibid.*, p. 753.

particular research, or because of confusion over time sequences, they seemed to be continuously describing very different groups and phenomena. In 1936, however, George Gallup began measuring the independent in national sample surveys by asking respondents to identify themselves as Republicans or Democrats or independents. His research standardized all future attempts to identify the so-called independent vote, and the survey tool (along with the self-classification techniques) has dominated political research ever since.

But the use of a self-administered definition to single out those who are independent of the two major political parties has resulted in all kinds of mischief. And once the surveys were begun, the theories built, and the subsequent modifications and other findings piled on top of the original research, the course was almost irreversible—particularly for those who had an investment in the original work. What has been produced is a set of generalizations and suppositions about independents built upon the original survey research efforts undertaken in the 1940's, refined and added to during the 1950's and 1960's.

The profile of the independent that finally emerged is best seen in the work done by a team at the Survey Research Center of the University of Michigan in their classic voting treatise, *The American Voter*.[3] The impact of their conclusions on other research and political thinking has been unequalled, for their conclusions tore up the traditional democratic rhetoric about the independent, rational citizen who decided American elections:

> The ideal of the Independent citizen, attentive to politics, concerned with the course of government, who weighs the rival appeals of a campaign and reaches a judgment that is unswayed by partisan prejudice, has had such a vigorous history in the tradition of political reform—and has such a hold on civic education today—that one could easily suppose that the habitual partisan has the more limited interest and concern

[3] Angus Campbell et al. (New York: Wiley, 1960). An earlier such analysis is *Voting: A Study of Opinion Formation in a Presidential Campaign*, B. R. Berelson et al. (Chicago: U. of Chicago Press, 1954). See also Peter H. Rossi, "Four Landmarks in Voting Research," in *American Voting Behavior*, ed. Eugene Burdick and Arthur T. Brodbeck (New York: Free Press, 1959).

with politics. But if the usual image of the Independent voter is intended as more than a normative ideal, it fits poorly the characteristics of the Independents in our samples. Far from being more attentive, interested and informed, *Independents* tend as a group to be somewhat less involved in politics. They have somewhat poorer knowledge of the issues, their image of the candidates is fainter, their interest in the campaign is less, their concern over the outcome is relatively slight, and their choice between competing candidates, although it is indeed made later in the campaign, seems much less to spring from discovered evaluations of the elements of national politics.[4]

But like others who have built their theories on this self-identified independent voter, the University of Michigan group is faced with explaining away the fact that these same marginal, uninformed, disinterested voters are the key to the decision-making process in American campaigns. This state of affairs has led to all sorts of mental gymnastics by American political scientists.[5] They are not alone. Some European and most British political scientists wrestle with the same dilemma. In countries other than the United States, particularly Great Britain, those who change from one party to another are called "floating voters." Mark Abrams believes they represent fully one-third of the electorate.[6] In a piece forecasting the 1964 election, Abrams asserted that the floater wants efficient government from the political parties and presumably makes up his mind on this score. He found the floaters to be fairly representative of the community in age, sex, class, and

[4] *The American Voter*, p. 83.

[5] In their *Measures of Political Attitudes* (Ann Arbor: U. of Michigan Survey Research Center, 1968), John P. Robinson et al. attempt to clarify this confusion but succeed only in compounding it: "While Democratic party identifiers outnumber Republican identifiers almost two to one (and among independents the Democratic "leaners" usually outnumber the Republican "leaners"), election results are much closer than this division of identification would indicate. Converse (1966) has examined this apparent paradox more fully within the framework of his normal vote concept. Because Republican identifiers are much more likely to turn out to vote than Democratic identifiers, the normal vote is around 54% Democratic to 46% Republican. This division of the vote, of course, assumes little visible difference between particular candidates" (p. 495).

[6] "What the Floating Voter Wants," *London Observer*, April 5, 1964.

other characteristics. There were but two exceptions: floaters tend to be the sons and daughters of parents uninterested in politics or they often "reach their position out of a desire to repudiate their own past." Many are of working-class origin but think of themselves as middle class. Floating voters also think that their independence represents political sophistication rather than indecisiveness or ignorance. But the facts do not support their belief, says Abrams. They are in actuality more ignorant than committed.

By now the Survey Research Center profile of the independent is established in the literature of political science and is accepted by political writers and observers everywhere. Jules Abels, for example, has said this:

> The independent voters, who for so long under democratic theory had been considered the most intelligent part of the electorate and the most virtuous beyond the call of tradition, are in reality the least interested, the least knowledgeable and the least intelligent.[7]

And Penn Kimball has concluded:

> ... the swing vote is substantially composed of voters with the lowest interest in politics. ... [They] are the most susceptible to the modern techniques for escalating emotional attitudes. ... [They are] the least educated and worst-off segment of the population, with little inclination to study political literature or to attend formal public meetings. ... [Their] reading habits are attuned to gossip columns. ...[8]

The exegesis of what were preliminary research findings has become accepted dogma.

SOME QUALMS ABOUT IT ALL

Very few political scientists have questioned the methodology of the self-administered definition and subsequent findings concerning independents. Three exceptions are

[7] *The Degeneration of Our Presidential Election* (New York: Macmillan, 1968), p. 69.

[8] *Bobby Kennedy and the New Politics* (Englewood Cliffs: Prentice Hall, 1968), p. 10.

cited here—one in 1952 and the others in 1961 and 1963.[9]
Only one of the three, V. O. Key, Jr., has not been ignored
by the political science community.

The first work to question the existing literature on the
independent was a study examining some of the statewide
elections held in 1950.[10] In this early attempt to identify
the independent voter, Alan S. Meyer looked for appropriate definitions of the independents, how they could be
located, what their characteristics might be, and how numerous they were. Their basic characteristic, Meyer determined, was that they were flexible with respect to political
parties. Political flexibility could mean inconsistency over
a period of time, withholding commitment to a party,
split-ticket voting, and disagreement with one's party line
on issues. He found that these measures of flexibility were
related.

Political involvement was the second dimension used to
test independence, and Meyer said that the independent
voter combines this involvement with nonpartisanship:
"The Independent voter, then, is a deviate in the electorate, for he violates the rule that partisanship goes with
involvement, non-partisanship with apathy. . . ."[11]

Meyer's studies of the 1950 state elections in Colorado,
Washington, Minnesota, and Iowa found independent
voters to have *high political involvement characteristics:*
they voted in large numbers, they liked to discuss politics,
they followed their candidates closely in the media and
were very knowledgeable about them, and they were very
interested in their candidate's winning. In those ways they
closely resembled partisans, but they differed from the
partisans in that they very seldom tried to convert others
to their political point of view. Meyer also noted that

> . . . independents gave more evidence of making *considered*
> choices than do any of the other types. They are most likely

[9] There has been more open questioning and criticism since then,
but only with unusual caution and circumspection. For example, see
"Images of Voting" by Peter B. Natchez in *Public Policy*, Summer
1970.

[10] Alan S. Meyer, "The Independent Voter," in *Public Opinion
and Congressional Elections*, ed. William N. McPhee and William
Glaser (New York: Free Press, 1962), pp. 66-67.

[11] *Ibid.*, p. 71.

of all voters to see merit in the programs of both parties, they are most likely to consider rival candidates, before making their choice, and they are most likely to split their tickets.[12]

Independent voting was seen by Meyer as a deviant and transitional phenomenon. It may arise out of social environments and political backgrounds that steer the voter into political activity, while at the same time providing contradictory pulls in regard to the direction of the activity. For these two reasons independent voting is an unstable position.[13] Meyer's overall findings concerning independent voters are very similar to our profile of the ticket-splitter.

The first systematic challenge to the existing concept of the independent voter appeared in 1961 in an obscure little book by Dr. H. Daudt.[14] Perhaps his findings and conclusions were initially discredited or ignored because of the enormity of their implications. To quote Philip E. Converse, who briefly mentioned and then dismissed this book, Daudt's "intensive review of the major voting studies asserts that none of the published data has adequately supported the notion of a 'floating voter,' much less any hypothesis as to his character."[15] Citing evidence from such classic voting studies as *Voting* and *The American Voter*, Daudt neatly disproves some of their major hypotheses about the floating voters (i.e., independents) by using their own published data.

Daudt brings to the data a behavioral definition which extends through time: "Floating voters do not make the same choice in two successive elections."[16] Using this definition, he finds that neither social background factors nor psychological variables can be used in differentiating

[12] *Ibid.*, pp. 73-74.

[13] *Ibid.*, p. 77.

[14] *Floating Voters & the Floating Vote: A Critical Analysis of American and English Election Studies* (Leiden, Holland: H. E. Stenfert, Kroese N. V., 1961).

[15] Angus Campbell, et al., *Elections and the Political Order* (New York: Wiley, 1966), p. 137.

[16] *Floating Voters*, p. 7.

Republicans, Democrats, and floating voters. Then he proceeds to his major conclusion and its implications: "It seems to me that this classic view is better suited to the election process than practitioners of empirical election research often suppose."[17]

After scoring the authors of *The American Voter* for not providing the statistics to justify the conclusion that shifts in party strength between elections occur among the less involved and poorly informed voters, Daudt ends his book by stating:

> The pertinacity of the myth of "dumbness" of the floating voters may perhaps also explain why so little attention has been paid to the types of floaters . . . but no survey-questionnaire has yet . . . contained the obvious question *why* has the voting choice been changed since the previous election? . . . Only for those who are of the opinion that floaters are less intelligent than the rest of the voting-age population is this omission unimportant.[18]

Daudt was right. Isolating the self-identified independent and putting him under the analytical microscope resulted in focusing research efforts on the study of party regulars and avoiding this key independent voting group.

V. O. Key, Jr., was undeniably a giant among political scientists, and his works in public opinion research and writing are a major contribution to the study of voting behavior. After a year in residence at the Survey Research Center at the University of Michigan, Key wrote a public opinion volume in 1961 which drew heavily—almost exclusively—on data of the Survey Research Center.[19] At the time of his death in 1963, he was working on a "little book"—as he called it—which had as its theme the "per-

[17] The classic view "implies that the policy of the government, the political issues, the parties' attitudes towards these, the activities of the parties, their programmes and their actions, will influence the voting choice, and that this choice is neither the outcome of group influences nor predictable with the aid of a few attributes."

[18] *Floating Voters*, p. 168.

[19] *Public Opinion and American Democracy* (New York: Knopf, 1967), 4th edition.

verse and unorthodox argument . . . that voters are not fools.''[20]

Key questioned the practice of analyzing aggregates consisting of large groups of people who had similar demographic and social characteristics (e.g., religion, occupation, place of residence, and education) and then providing statistical correlations to prove relationships between these determinants and voting behavior. He argued rather that voters' attitudes toward the issues, the candidates, and the parties are what is needed to understand elections.

Key also questioned those political observers who find the election of the President irrational since one party tends to stay in power over a long period of time. This, to the cynics, suggests simple, repetitive voting. Key asserted—and our ticket-splitting data supports his hypothesis—that what appears to be a stable majority keeping one party in power is in fact a *highly fluid majority made up of majorities of the moment* (ad hoc majorities) created by voters' reactions.

Most important to our discussion are Key's comments on the nature of partisans and independents. He reviewed those voting study findings which conclude that the straight party voters (standpatters) are more interested and intelligent than the independents (switchers), who are allegedly the least interested and inconsistent in their attitudes and behavior. Reexamining the evidence found in the national surveys by Gallup, the Survey Research Center, and the election statistics, Key developed a different concept of the switch voter, or one who *changes his party vote* (i.e., splits his ticket) from one election to the next *rather than* changes *his views* during the course of a campaign. He found that in fact the switchers are *not* less informed and involved than standpatters, nor do they differ in terms of education and other factors thought associated with straight party voters:

> We have established patterns of movement of party switchers from election to election and the patterns of stability of the standpatter that lead us to a conception of the voter that is not often propounded. From our analysis the voter merges as a

[20] *The Responsible Electorate,* written with the assistance of Milton C. Cummings, Jr. (New York: Random House, 1968), p. 7.

person who appraises the actions of government, who has policy preferences and who relates his vote to those appraisals and preferences.[21]

Voters, particularly those who switch, make their decisions on the basis of their perception and evaluation of the policies and performance of government. The classical conception of the apathetic independent voter did not fit Key's analysis.

It is interesting to note that the Survey Research Center did eventually acknowledge Key's theory of rational voting in their 1968 election summary report and termed it "The Key Corrective." In the Center's own words, the

... 1968 [election] seems to be a prototypical case of the election that does not produce many changes of policy preferences but does permit electors to sort themselves and the candidates into groups of substantial homogeneity on matters of public policy. This trend over the course of the campaign calls to mind the posthumous contention of V. O. Key, *The Responsible Electorate*, that the mass electorate is a good deal less irrational, ill-informed or sheep-like than it had become fashionable to suppose. He presented empirical materials to develop a counter-image of "an electorate moved by concern about control and relevant questions of public policy, of governmental performance, and of executive personality." To our point of view, Key's general thesis represented a welcome corrective on some earlier emphases. . . .[22]

A new definition of "independence" in voting has long been needed.

INDEPENDENCE IN VOTING—
A NEW DEFINITION

Political scientists and public survey research firms such as the Gallup Poll have described the independent's atti-

[21] *Ibid.*, pp. 58-59.
[22] *American Political Science Review*, December 1969, p. 1095.

tudes and voting behavior in scores of professional articles and reports. However, the difficulty with these descriptions is that the independent voter is always defined in terms of his own or others' perceptions and the definition is not anchored to actual voting behavior. The typical question used in self-administered definitions is this: "Do you consider yourself a Republican or a Democrat?" If the answer is "independent" or "don't know," the questionnaire usually probes further: "Do you lean toward the Republican Party or the Democratic?" Variations of this might be: "Would you consider yourself a strong Republican, a weak Republican, an independent Republican, an independent, an independent Democrat, a weak Democrat, a strong Democrat?" The semantic differential technique is another device that has been introduced in recent years to determine the strength of party identification.

THE PROBLEM

But while the political scientist and other scholars in social psychology may find it interesting to know how a voter identifies himself, this does not help him explain how the voter's total voting behavior is related to his self-perceptions. The voter must be asked how he actually behaves in the voting booth—and with respect to all major political offices, not just the Presidency. The traditional measurement of party identification as the major determinant of voting has not been as precise and as meaningful as some would have us believe. If a questionnaire is to determine true independence, it must ask the voter not how he identifies himself but how he actually voted. A procedure like that below should be adopted:

> Now, I would like to ask you a few questions about the elections that were just held.
> First of all, let me hand you a card which shows some of the offices that were up for election this fall. Please give me the alphabetical letter that corresponds to your vote at that time.

	Republican A	Democrat B	Other C	Don't Know D
U.S. President	☐	☐	☐	☐
U.S. Senator	☐	☐	☐	☐
Governor	☐	☐	☐	☐
U.S. Congressman	☐	☐	☐	☐
Secretary of State	☐	☐	☐	☐
Attorney-General	☐	☐	☐	☐
State Treasurer	☐	☐	☐	☐

(If respondent cannot remember, provide names of candidates.)

	A	B	C
President	Nixon	Humphrey	Wallace
U. S. Senator	Tower	Carr	
Governor	Milliken	Levin	
Congressman	Collins	Pool	
Secretary of State	Smith	Jones	
Attorney-General	Martin	Stewart	
State Treasurer	Fay	James	

With the foregoing measurement technique (sometimes using an actual sealed ballot for the respondent to fill out), one can now establish a new typology of voting based upon actual behavior: behavioral strong Republicans, behavioral weak Republicans, behavioral Ticket-splitters, behavioral weak Democrats, and behavioral strong Democrats. The following illustrations depict this concept.

SUMMARY OF HYPOTHETICAL RESULTS
USING BEHAVIORAL APPROACH ONLY

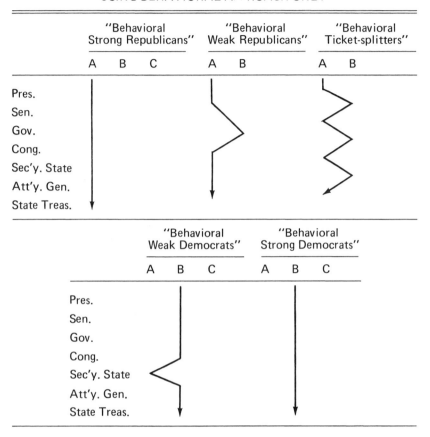

The inadequacies in the self-perception school of thought are clearly demonstrated in the 1968 post-election study by the Gallup Poll. Forty-five percent of those voters who said they were Republicans actually reported that they voted a split ticket. Forty-seven percent of those voters who claimed they were Democrats also voted a split ticket. To further widen the discrepancy between self-perception and actual behavior, one-fourth of the self-classified independents voted a straight party ticket.

Much of the time, then, self-perception will fail even to identify the Democrats and the Republicans. Many voters who consider themselves Republicans or Democrats (even strong ones) will split their tickets in a variety of elections. Unless one asks the direction of their voting acts in specific election contexts, he cannot know whether his descriptions of strong or behavioral partisans are accurate and relevant.

An Illinois post-election study conducted in December of 1968 illustrates the problems of definition:

TABLE 6

Perception and Behavior	%
Self-Perception[23]	
Republican	31.4
Democrat	46.4
Other, "Independent," Don't know	22.2
	100.0
Actual Voting Behavior[24]	
Voted Republican ticket	31.1
Voted Democratic ticket	37.7
Voted split tickets	31.2
	100.0

Considerably more voters perceived themselves as Democrats (46.4%) than actually voted that way (37.7%). In 1968 the State of Illinois voted for a Republican President (Richard Nixon), for a Republican U. S. Senator (Everett Dirksen) and for a Republican Governor (Richard Oglivie); yet, nearly half the Illinois voters thought of themselves as Democrats. Combined, the statistics for self-perception and those for actual behavior yield the following table:

[23] Determined by asking "Do you consider yourself a Republican, a Democrat, or what?"

[24] Determined by asking how respondent voted for a number of offices on the ballot in 1968.

TABLE 7

1968 ILLINOIS POST-ELECTION SURVEY[25]
(N = 800)

Self-Perception	Actual Voting Behavior (100.0%)		
	Straight Republican (31.1%)	Split Ticket (31.2%)	Straight Democrat (37.7%)
Republican . . . . . . (31.4%)	79.4	21.7	1.1
Democrat . . . . (46.4%)	5.6	34.0	91.4
Independent, Other (22.2%)	15.0	44.3	7.5
State Electorate. . .(100.0%)	100.0	100.0	100.0

Many more voters split their tickets than consider themselves independents. Note that only 44.3% of those who are behavioral ticket-splitters perceived themselves as independents. Thirty-four percent saw themselves as Democrats and 21.7% of the independents thought of themselves as Republicans.

Other opinion studies have yielded similar results. A national research study in July 1967 by Market Opinion Research (Table 8) found that about 13% of the behavioral Republicans consider themselves independents as do 13%

TABLE 8

1967 NATIONAL SURVEY

Self-Perception	Actual Voting Behavior[26]			
	Straight Republican	Split Ticket	Straight Democrat	Other
Republican . . . . (25.7%)	79.3	19.3	2.2	17.0
Democrat . . . . . (44.9%)	5.5	32.7	81.5	43.5
Independent . . . (25.1%)	13.5	43.5	13.4	31.4
Other, Don't know (4.3%)	1.7	4.5	2.9	8.1
Total National Electorate (100.0%)	100.0	100.0	100.0	100.0

[25] Market Opinion Research, Detroit, Michigan.

[26] Determined by asking how respondents voted in 1966 for U.S. Senator, U. S. Congressman, state governor, etc.

of the behavioral Democrats. Almost 20% of the ticket-splitters think of themselves as Republicans—so over half of the ticket-splitters consider themselves Republicans or Democrats rather than independents.

In summary, 26% of those who voted either straight Democratic or straight Republican saw themselves as independents, while 52% of the ticket-splitters thought of themselves as Republicans or Democrats, with twice as many in the former category as in the latter. See chart below:

How Actual Voters Consider Themselves (1967)

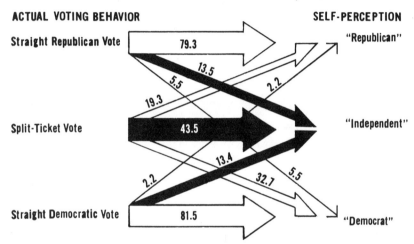

SUMMARY

By using only the self-administered and hence self-perceived definition of "Do you consider yourself a Republican, Democrat, or independent?", political scientists and public pollsters have offered only a partial explanation of independence in voting. The disparity between the perceptual approach and the behavioral approach has inevitably created misunderstandings about contemporary voting behavior. Many Republicans, and Democrats, split their ballots regularly while many so-called independents are disguised partisans.

Only by modifying our current methodology for identifying behavioral patterns will we be able to better describe elections. The next step in political research is to develop hypotheses concerning these actual behavioral patterns. A new typology of voters is needed.

CHAPTER 3

The Socio-economic Characteristics
of the Ticket-splitter

But who are these changers, these floating voters? Do they
perhaps form certain distinguishable social groupings upon
which political factors exercise an influence by which they
induce a change of vote? Are they those persons within the
various social groupings who do not conform to political
group-norms because of cross-pressures? Or, are they perhaps
those voters [in whom] free discussion and the formation of
political opinions . . . play a greater role than in the lives of
others? H. Daudt, *Floating Voters and*
the Floating Vote (1961), p. 4

Thus far we have shown that ticket-splitting is on the
increase. We also believe that there is not a high correlation
between the so-called independents and actual ticket-
splitters. We have also demonstrated that measurement
techniques and conceptual formulations have caused most
of the confusion. What is needed now is the answer to this
question: "If the ticket-splitter is actually an amalgam of
independents, Republicans, and Democrats, can one define
separate characteristics for him and can he be traced
through time?"

Unfortunately, little research has been conducted in this
area.[1] Some of the first data on the psychological char-

[1] Angus Campbell and Warren Miller, "The Motivational Basis of
Straight and Split-Ticket Voting," *American Political Science Review* (June 1957): "The fact of ballot splitting in American elections
is of course a commonplace, but it has not been widely studied and
it is not well understood" (p. 293).

acteristics of the ticket-splitter was provided by the Survey
Research Center in an article on ticket-splitting:

> ... when the voter's candidate preference and issue partisan-
> ship conflict with his sense of party attachment he tends to try
> to satisfy *both* components of the conflict by supporting
> candidates from both parties. His conflicting motivations re-
> duce the pressure toward a party-oriented vote and open the
> way to a divided ballot.[2]

The motivated split-ticket voter, contends the Survey Research Center, is politically involved, but his political
motives are in conflict and his split-ticket is therefore a
compromise.

Regrettably, however, the Survey Research Center article told us little about any socio-economic characteristics
that mark the ticket-splitter. The only variable that they
found was that metropolitan, as opposed to rural, areas
had a low incidence of ticket-splitting and that within the
metropolitan areas suburbs contained the *lowest* level. This
data, gleaned from their 1956 Presidential study, is at odds
with our recent studies. We found that ticket-splitting
increases as one moves from the core city to the suburbs.

The Gallup post-election survey in 1968 isolated more
socio-economic characteristics of the split-ticket voter.
However, one must bear in mind that Gallup's definition
of ticket-splitting was obtained by asking the respondent:
"Did you vote for the candidate of *different* parties?"
Since his definition was a self-classified one and by personal testimony only, his results tended to follow "classic
independent" expectations.

Moreover, Gallup's straight-ticket voter tended to follow
the classic bloc-vote partisan: largely uneducated, over
fifty years old, residing in a large urban city in the East,
and having an income below $5,000. Thus, Gallup's recent
research effort into the realm of the split-ticket voter
yielded no startling information and, in fact, appeared to
reset the traditional sterotyped profile of the poorly educated voter of the masses (straight ticket) and the highly
educated, discriminating independent (i.e., a voter for can-

[2] *Ibid.*, pp. 296-297.

Self-perceived Ticket-splitter (Ranked)	% Margin exceeding national estimate
A political "Independent"	+ 18
Young adult (21-29 yrs.)	+ 12
College graduate	+ 10
White-collar occupation	+ 9
Professional & business occupation	+ 8
$10,000 & over income	+ 6
& 7,000 & over income	+ 6
Middle-aged adult (30-49 yrs.)	+ 5
High school graduate	+ 4
Western United States resident	+ 4
Midwestern United States resident	+ 3
Medium-size urban cities (50-500,000) ..	+ 3
Rural areas	+ 3

didates of "different" parties). The Survey Research Center studies had painted almost the opposite picture of the party identifier and the independent in their book, *The American Voter*, about eight years earlier.

TABLE 9

THE SELF-CLASSIFIED TICKET-SPLITTER IN 1968: GALLUP POST-ELECTION SURVEY

Question: "For the various political offices, did you vote for all the candidates of one party—that is, a straight ticket—or did you vote for the candidates of different parties?"

	November, 1968		
	Straight	Different	Don't Know
National	43%	54%	3%
Sex			
Men	43	55	2
Women	43	53	4
Race			
White	42	55	3
Non-White	X	X	X

TABLE 9 (Continued)

	Straight	Different	Don't Know
Education			
College	34	64	2
High School	40	58	2
Grade School	61	34	5
Occupation			
Prof. & Bus.	35	62	3
White Collar	35	63	2
Farmers	43	54	3
Manual	44	53	3
Age			
21-29 years	32	66	2
30-49 years	39	59	2
50 & over	50	46	4
Religion			
Protestant	44	53	3
Catholic	43	53	4
Jewish	X	X	X
Politics			
Republican	53	45	2
Democrat	49	47	4
Independent	25	72	3
Region			
East	46	50	4
Midwest	41	57	2
South	43	53	4
West	40	58	2
Income			
$10,000 & over	38	60	2
$ 7,000 & over	38	60	2
$ 5,000 - $6,999	41	53	6
$ 3,000 - $4,999	50	48	2
Under $3,000	57	37	6
Community Size			
1,000,000 & over	49	49	2
500,000 & over	49	49	2
50,000 - 499,999	41	57	2
2,500 - 49,999	39	56	5
Under 2,500, Rural	39	57	4

A more pertinent analysis of the ticket-splitter was made in 1967 by a Romney for President committee. This study found that the national ticket-splitter had a good many of the characteristics attributed to the Republican voter, though he was somewhat younger, more often Catholic, more often a suburbanite or resident of a middle-size city, and a member of a larger family.

THE NATIONAL TICKET-SPLITTER PROFILE
(N = 1169)

High school graduate
Some college, graduate or post-graduate
High and middle income ($7,000-$24,999)
Younger (21-29 years) and middle years (30-59)
Professional/technical
Managers/officials/owners
Clerical/sales workers
Operatives and kindred workers
Nonunion
Male
American born white
Protestant but also somewhat Catholic
Married
Community Size: 2,500 to 499,999
Family Size: 3, 4, 5, 6
Homeowner

Our own data suggests that the ticket-splitter is slightly younger, somewhat more educated, somewhat more white-collar, and more suburban than the typical middle-class voter. In addition, the ticket-splitter tends to consume more media output about politics and is more active politically than the straight Democrat (but less than the straight Republican).

To confirm these generalizations, note the differences between ticket-splitters and the party partisans in Table 10, which is based on a national sample taken in 1967 by Market Opinion Research, Inc.

TABLE 10

NATIONAL SOCIAL/ECONOMIC PROFILES OF BEHAVIORAL
REPUBLICANS, DEMOCRATS, AND TICKET-SPLITTERS (1967)
(N = 1169)

Socio-economic Characteristics	National Voting Behavior			
	Repub-lican	Ticket-splitter	Demo-crat	Total
Education				
Grade school or less	14.3%	18.2%	34.5%	22.9%
Some high school	16.0	16.0	18.2	17.9
Graduate high school	31.5	33.8	28.9	31.9
Some college	21.4	16.4	11.5	15.4
Graduate college	11.3	8.2	4.5	7.3
Post-graduate work	4.6	7.1	2.0	3.8
DK	.8	.4	.6	.9
Income				
0-$2,999	8.8	11.2	20.7	14.5
$3,000-$4,999	13.9	11.2	17.9	14.3
$5,000-$5,999	11.8	6.3	8.7	9.7
$6,000-$6,999	8.4	10.4	11.2	10.5
$7,000-$9,999	19.7	23.8	20.4	22.6
$10,000-$14,999	21.8	25.7	11.5	16.4
$15,000-$24,999	8.4	4.8	3.9	4.6
$25,000 and over	2.9	1.5	1.4	1.8
DK	4.2	5.2	4.2	5.6
Age				
18-20 years	.4	-	-	.2
21-29 years	9.2	15.2	10.4	13.7
30-39 years	18.5	21.2	17.9	20.1
40-49 years	14.3	20.8	18.5	18.0
50-59 years	21.8	21.6	20.4	19.7
60-64 years	6.3	7.1	8.1	7.3
65 years and over	29.4	14.1	24.6	21.1
Occupation				
Not in labor force	29.8	33.1	37.0	36.7
Professional/technical	11.8	13.8	3.1	7.9
Farm owners/managers	4.6	.4	.6	1.4
Managers/officials/owners	7.1	6.3	5.0	5.6

TABLE 10 (Continued)

Socio-economic Characteristics	Republican	Ticket-splitter	Democrat	Total
		National Voting Behavior		
Clerical/sales workers	9.2	16.4	10.9	10.9
Skilled craftsmen/foremen	5.9	6.3	8.4	7.0
Operatives and kindred workers	5.5	8.2	5.3	6.7
Service and household workers				
and laborers	8.4	5.9	14.3	10.4
Farm laborers/foremen	.4	-	.6	.4
Retired	17.2	9.7	14.8	12.9
Union Member				
Yes	16.0	19.7	26.1	20.3
No	84.0	80.3	73.9	79.7
Sex				
Male	49.2	42.8	41.7	42.5
Female	50.8	57.2	58.3	57.5
Race and National Origin				
American Born White	92.0	92.2	78.2	85.4
Negro Born	4.2	5.6	13.7	9.3
Foreign Born	3.8	2.2	8.1	5.3
Religion				
Protestant	79.0	57.6	56.3	63.8
Catholic	14.7	34.2	32.8	27.0
Jewish	1.7	3.7	5.3	3.4
Greek Orthodox	-	.4	.6	.4
None	.4	.4	1.1	1.0
All other	4.2	3.7	3.9	4.4
Marital Status				
Married/separated	74.4	83.3	77.6	78.4
Single	8.0	5.9	6.2	6.9
Divorced	4.6	1.9	1.4	2.2
Widow/widower	13.0	8.9	14.8	12.4
Community Size—Place of Residence				
1,000,000 and over	8.0	6.3	9.2	8.8
500,000 to 999,999	5.0	7.8	10.1	7.8
50,000 to 499,999	26.9	26.4	25.2	26.0
2,500 to 49,999	33.2	35.7	30.0	31.1

TABLE 10 (Continued)

Socio-economic Characteristics	National Voting Behavior			
	Repub-lican	Ticket-splitter	Demo-crat	Total
Under 2,500—rural	20.6	17.1	14.3	17.7
DK	6.3	6.7	11.2	8.6
Family Size				
One	17.6	8.9	16.2	14.1
Two	31.1	27.5	29.4	29.1
Three	16.4	16.7	15.1	16.2
Four	16.8	23.4	12.3	17.4
Five	8.8	13.8	13.4	12.2
Six	5.5	5.9	5.0	5.6
Seven	2.1	1.9	3.1	2.3
Eight	.8	.4	2.2	1.2
Nine or more	.8	1.5	3.1	2.0
Status of Dwelling				
Owner	80.7	77.7	70.3	72.0
Rent	19.3	21.9	29.7	27.4

Using the data in Table 10, we can draw the following graphs plotting the relative positions of the three types of voters against the national estimate for the total electorate with respect to the key socio-economic considerations we have singled out.

EDUCATIONAL ATTAINMENT

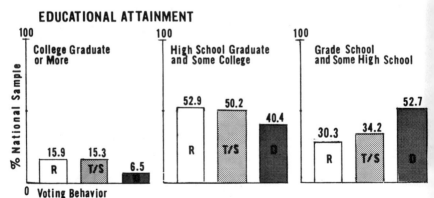

FAMILY INCOME

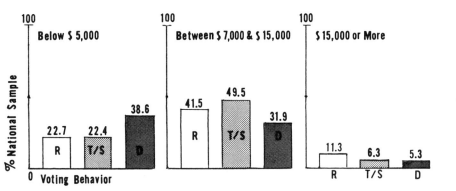

AGE GROUPS

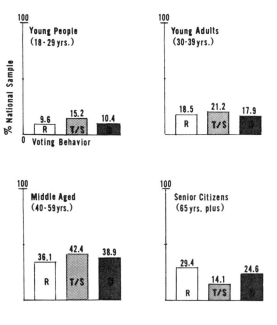

OCCUPATIONAL LEVELS

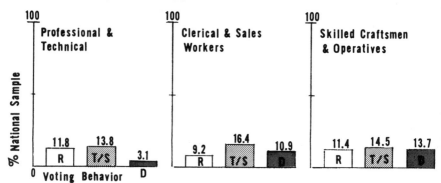

SEX

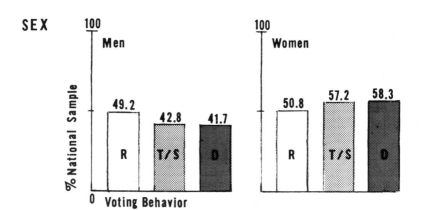

RELIGION

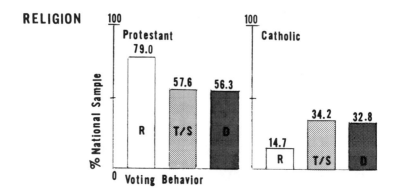

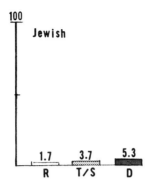

INDEPENDENTS AND TICKET-SPLITTERS

The self-classified independent and the ticket-splitter are not fully one and the same voter. In fact, in comparing the socio-economic profiles of the two in the state of Michigan, we found that the so-called independent and the ticket-splitter were in many ways the complete opposite of each other. The significant differences we observed are these:

INDEPENDENT VOTING

Self-identified independent	Ticket-splitter
50-59 years of age	30-49 years of age
Female	Male
Protestant	Catholic
Union/Skilled workers	Managers/Owners
Low income ($3,000-$5,000)	Middle Income ($7,500-$15,000)

From these generalizations one can readily see that a campaign strategy designed to capture the "independent or swing vote" as defined by self-identification might very well misappropriate valuable campaign resources and work.

In Table 11 below, notice the large differences in some of the categories not only between the nominal independents and the ticket-splitters, but also between the self-perceived and the behavioral Democrats and Republicans.

TABLE 11

SOCIO-ECONOMIC PROFILES OF MICHIGAN VOTERS (1965)

| (N = 602) | | Respondents: Perception and Behavior | | | | | |
| | | Republican | | Independent | | Democrat | |
Socio-economic Characteristics	Total	Per-ceived	Behav-ioral	Ind.	T-S	Per-ceived	Behav-ioral
Income							
0-$2,999	9.6%	8.7%	7.2%	5.5%	6.6%	13.4%	11.5%
$3,000-$4,999	10.3	5.1	6.0	12.5	6.6	11.5	12.9
$5,000-$7,499	29.2	29.0	31.3	29.0	29.9	29.1	29.7
$7,500-$9,999	24.8	27.5	25.3	29.5	32.7	19.5	22.9
$10,000-$14,999	15.8	21.0	19.3	17.5	19.6	11.9	10.4
$15,000 and over	8.5	8.0	8.5	4.0	3.7	12.3	10.8
Refused	1.8	.7	2.4	2.0	.9	2.3	1.8
Age							
21-29 years	13.0	15.9	12.0	15.0	14.0	10.0	12.2
30-39 years	25.4	23.2	24.1	23.0	28.0	28.7	25.8
40-49 years	27.7	27.6	27.7	26.0	31.8	29.1	27.6
50-59 years	18.8	15.9	16.9	24.0	18.7	16.1	19.3
60 years and over	15.1	17.4	19.3	12.0	7.5	16.1	15.1
Occupation							
Skilled craftsmen/foremen and kindred workers	17.6	12.3	14.5	20.0	14.1	18.8	20.4
Professional/technical	15.1	19.6	18.7	14.0	15.9	13.8	13.6
Managers/officials business owners	14.4	21.7	19.9	11.0	16.8	13.0	11.1
Clerical and kindred workers	14.4	17.4	13.3	15.0	18.7	12.6	13.6
Operatives and kindred workers	11.5	8.7	10.8	12.0	8.4	12.6	12.5

Service workers/private household laborers	11.5	7.3	6.0	13.5	13.1	11.9	13.3
Retired	8.5	8.0	10.8	7.0	5.6	9.6	7.9
Housewife/student	3.0	3.6	2.4	3.0	4.7	2.7	2.2
Unemployed	2.7	.7	1.8	3.0	.9	3.4	4.3
Farm owners and managers	.8	—	.6	1.5	.9	.8	1.1
Don't know	.5	.7	1.2	—	.9	.8	—
Union Member							
Yes	35.0	16.7	22.3	38.5	29.9	42.1	45.9
No	65.0	83.3	77.7	61.5	70.1	57.9	54.1
Sex							
Male	51.0	49.3	44.0	47.5	55.1	54.8	54.1
Female	49.0	50.7	56.0	52.5	44.9	45.2	45.9
Race and National Origin							
American-born white	85.2	93.5	94.6	89.0	94.4	77.8	76.3
Negro-born	8.8	2.2	1.2	8.0	3.7	13.0	15.1
Foreign-born	6.0	4.3	4.2	3.0	1.9	9.2	8.6
Religion							
Protestant	59.3	81.9	79.5	67.0	60.8	41.4	48.4
Catholic	28.4	15.2	16.3	26.0	34.6	37.5	32.2
Jewish	9.0	2.2	2.4	3.0	2.8	17.2	15.4
Greek Orthodox	.3	—	—	—	—	.8	.4
None	1.7	—	1.2	3.0	.9	1.5	1.8
Other	1.3	.7	.6	1.0	.9	1.5	1.8
How Father Voted							
Republican	26.4	63.0	54.8	24.5	30.9	8.0	9.0
Democrat	43.8	12.3	19.3	36.5	38.3	66.3	62.7
Ticket-splitter	14.5	14.5	13.9	24.5	21.5	6.9	10.7
Don't know	15.3	10.1	12.0	14.5	9.3	18.8	17.6

The following graphs present selected categories from Table 11 pictorially, plotting the relative positions of the nominal independent, the ticket-splitter, and the perceived and actual Republican and Democrat against the national estimate for that category.

MICHIGAN VOTERS

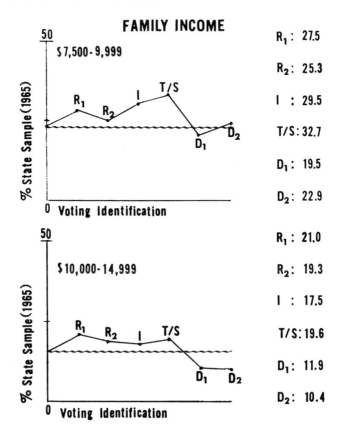

FAMILY INCOME

R_1 : 27.5

R_2 : 25.3

I : 29.5

T/S: 32.7

D_1 : 19.5

D_2 : 22.9

R_1 : 21.0

R_2 : 19.3

I : 17.5

T/S: 19.6

D_1 : 11.9

D_2 : 10.4

Legend:

R_1- Republicans (perceived)   I - Independents (perceived)
R_2-Republicans (actual behavior) D_1 - Democrats (perceived)
T/S - Ticket-Splitters (actual behavior) D_2- Democrats (actual behavior)

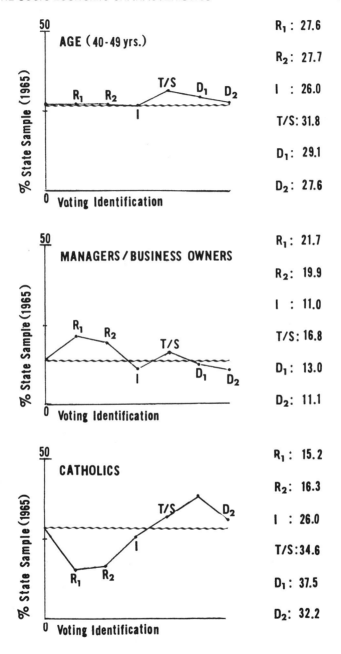

AGE (40-49 yrs.)

% State Sample (1965)

0 Voting Identification

R₁ : 27.6

R₂ : 27.7

I : 26.0

T/S: 31.8

D₁ : 29.1

D₂ : 27.6

MANAGERS / BUSINESS OWNERS

% State Sample (1965)

0 Voting Identification

R₁ : 21.7

R₂ : 19.9

I : 11.0

T/S: 16.8

D₁ : 13.0

D₂ : 11.1

CATHOLICS

% State Sample (1965)

0 Voting Identification

R₁ : 15.2

R₂ : 16.3

I : 26.0

T/S:34.6

D₁ : 37.5

D₂ : 32.2

SUMMARY

The overlap between the traditionally classified independent and the actual ticket-splitter is only about one-half. The ticket-splitter is more likely than the self-classified independent to be politically active, is in the age range of about 30 to 50 years, is in the middle-income bracket ($10,000-$15,000), is a male in the professional and technical positions, and is more Catholic than the behavioral Republican but less so than the behavioral Democrat.

Now that we have some picture of the ticket-splitter and his characteristics vis-à-vis the independent, how can this knowledge be put to use? We know that the split-ticket voter is, most of the time, the balance of power in elections and makes up about one-fourth (or more) of the total electorate. In close elections or in localities where one party has a smaller core strength than the dominant party, the ticket-splitter is the key to any major election.

CHAPTER 4

The Political Decision-making Processes of the Ticket-splitter

... Polls and television have already induced massive indirect effects upon the political process in America and undoubtedly will continue to influence the political process in the future.... Polls and television have modified and reshaped our expectations of political candidates.... They are making fundamental changes in the traditional national political party structures and function.... They have introduced new techniques of mass persuasion into the political process.... In short, they have been instrumental in the emergence of a new politics on the American scene....

Harold Mendelsohn & Irving Crespi,
Polls, Television, and the New Politics
(1970), p. 7

In the ideal campaign, a nearly flawless, up-to-date, two-way communications system exists between the candidate and the voter and the candidate is able to respond sensitively to the information that comes in. The efficient campaign today allocates resources—money, time, and energy—to meet the candidate's communications objectives, whether those be to influence the ticket-splitter or straight party voter. In short, we believe that the campaign process is best understood as an information and communications system.

Among all the major factors entering into the decision-making process of an election, political analysts have believed the most important to be party identification, group affiliations (religion, union, occupation, etc.), which reflect socio-economic status, the candidates themselves, and finally the issues. But in the survey studies that we have conducted or reviewed over the last several elections, the dominance of party identification has evaporated. Today when people are asked how they make up their minds about a candidate, they discuss his general ability, his personality, his ability to handle the job, his stand on the issues, and so on.[1] This is especially true for the split-ticket voter. Yet, many political scientists (especially those who are far removed from the realities of actual campaigning) still persist in teaching students and telling journalists that people make up their minds mainly on the basis of party identification. The shift in priorities that has occurred is presented in Table 12.

TABLE 12

HOW VOTERS MAKE UP THEIR MINDS ABOUT CANDIDATES[2]

Currently (1960-)	Recent Past (through approximately 1960)

1. Candidates
   personality
   ability to handle the job
	1. Party

2. Issues
   candidates' stands
   candidates' and party's ability
      to handle problems
	2. Group Affiliations

3. Party
   identification
   membership
	3. Candidates

4. Group Affiliations
   religious
   ethnic
   occupational
	4. Issues

[1] Open-end question from a 1970 Michigan study done for Governor William G. Milliken by Market Opinion Research. "As you think about how you make up your mind when you decide to vote for a candidate, what are the most important things that come to mind?"

[2] Based on the 1970 Market Opinion Research study.

MEDIA PATTERNS

Since what is of primary importance to the ticket-splitter is information about the candidate and his views on the issues, he relies heavily on the media. In this study, a communications medium is defined as any instrument that conducts information, whether it be family, friends, television, radio, or organizations.

In a 1970 election survey conducted in Michigan, voters were asked to examine a list of thirty-five variables that might have some impact on the way they made up their minds about political matters. The respondents in the survey then rated each one of these variables on an eleven-point scale. Table 13 presents the results obtained from two voting groups—undecided voters in the 1970 gubernatorial contest and ticket-splitters.

Examine those that are 5.0 points or higher. Among the interpersonal media, contacts with the candidates and talks with their families ranked high. Among the audio-visual media, the first five variables are all above five percentage points. Among the audio media, only radio educational programs and radio newscasts are above five points. Among the print media, only newspaper editorials and newspaper stories are over the five-point mark. In the organizational category, only the Democratic Party had a five-point rating.

TABLE 13

RELATIVE IMPORTANCE OF FACTORS THAT INFLUENCED
THE VOTING DECISIONS OF 1970 GUBERNATORIAL
UNDECIDEDS AND TICKET-SPLITTERS IN MICHIGAN[3]
(May, 1970: N = 809)

Media	Guber-natorial undecided	Ticket-splitters
Inter-personal		
Talks with family	5.5	5.6
Contacts with candidates	5.0	5.2
Talks with friends	4.8	5.0
Talks with political party workers	4.3	4.2

[3] Market Opinion Research.

TABLE 13 (Continued)

Media	Guber-natorial undecided	Ticket-splitters
Talks with work associates	4.3	4.3
Talks with neighbors	3.8	3.9
Audio-visual		
Television newscasts	6.7	6.8
Television documentaries and specials	6.5	6.6
Television editorials	5.7	5.6
Television talk shows	5.6	5.6
Television educational programs	5.6	5.9
Television advertisements	3.6	3.6
Television entertainers	2.6	2.5
Movies	1.8	1.8
Stage plays	1.4	1.4
Audio		
Radio educational programs	5.3	5.5
Radio newscasts	5.3	5.5
Radio talk shows	4.5	4.9
Radio editorials	4.2	4.5
Telephone campaign messages	2.3	2.0
Phonograph records	1.3	1.1
Print		
Newspaper editorials	5.8	5.9
Newspaper stories	5.8	6.0
Magazine editorials	4.3	4.2
Political brochures	3.8	3.6
Magazine stories	3.8	4.0
Newspaper advertisements	3.8	3.7
Books	3.6	3.6
Political mailings	3.4	3.3
Magazine advertisements	2.9	2.6
Billboards	2.4	2.1
Organizational		
The Democratic Party	5.3	4.5
The Republican Party	3.6	4.1
Membership in religious organizations	3.4	3.1
Membership in professional or business organizations	3.2	3.4

The next table, Table 14, presents the data on Michigan ticket-splitters in a little different form. The factors that may influence the voting decision are ordered under three different headings according to whether they are "very important" (5.0 and over), "important" (3.0-4.9), or "not important" (1.0-2.9). Each of these lists is in turn ordered from most to least important.

TABLE 14
RELATIVE IMPORTANCE OF FACTORS THAT INFLUENCED THE VOTING DECISIONS OF TICKET-SPLITTERS IN MICHIGAN
(May, 1970: N = 809)

Very Important (5.0 & over)	Important (3.0-4.9)	Not Important (1.0-2.9)
Television newscasts	Radio talk shows	*Magazine advertisements
Television documentaries and specials	The Democratic Party	Television entertainers
Newspaper stories	Radio editorials	*Billboards
Newspaper editorials	Talks with work associates	*Telephone campaign messages
Television educational programs	Magazine editorials	Movies
Television editorials	*Talks with political party workers	Stage plays
Television talk shows	The Republican Party	Phonograph records
Talks with family	Magazine stories	
Radio educational programs	Talks with neighbors	
Radio newscasts	*Newspaper advertisements	
*Contacts with candidates	*Political brochures	
Talks with friends	*Television advertisements	
	Books	
	Membership in professional or business organizations	
	*Political mailings	
	Membership in religious organizations	

*Factors which can be influenced or controlled by the candidate.

Contacts with candidates, talks with political workers, political brochures, newspaper advertisements, television advertisements, political mailings, magazine advertisements, billboards, and telephone campaign messages are nine media that can be directly controlled or in some way manipulated by the campaign. They can be controlled in the sense that they can be purchased or that the energies of the candidate can be focused on them. But note that eleven of the twelve "very important" variables are really not controllable by the campaign strategists. The only one that can be controlled is "contacts with candidates." There are no advertisements in this "very important" group.[4]

Television news and documentaries and other specials were by far the most important media influences on the split-ticket voter, and newspaper stories and editorials rank third and fourth. Television educational programs are next, followed by television editorials and talk shows. Among all types of advertising, brochures ranked twenty-third in importance for the ticket-splitter; newspaper ads, twenty-second; television ads, twenty-fourth; mail, twenty-seventh; magazine ads, twenty-ninth; billboards, thirty-first; and telephone campaign messages, thirty-second.

What are most important, then, are those variables which cannot be directly controlled by the candidates. Thus any major campaign communications effort directed toward the ticket-splitter must go through media that cannot be completely controlled (i.e., purchased) by the candidates.

MEDIA USE AND SELECTION

A national survey conducted in July of 1967 for the Romney for President campaign reflected the way Republicans, Democrats and ticket-splitters use the various communication input systems for political information.

As Table 15 exhibits, the survey found that ticket-

[4] These data are at complete odds with the central thesis of *The Selling of the President,* by Joe McGinniss, as well as with the implicit intent behind the campaign spending limitation legislation being considered by Congress.

splitters and Republicans showed the greatest interest in reading newspaper campaign stories, while Democrats showed the least. A ten-point spread separated the Democrats from the other two behavioral groups.

TABLE 15

NATIONAL VOTER INTEREST IN CAMPAIGN STORIES
IN NEWSPAPERS: 1967[5]

(N = 1169)

	National Voting Behavior			
Read Campaign News Stories	Republican	Ticket-splitter	Democrat	Total
HIGH				
Every day without fail	30.8%	27.5%	24.6%	25.3%
Almost every day	33.3	37.2	30.8	31.0
(HIGH total)	64.1	64.7	55.4	56.3
MEDIUM				
Once or twice a week	13.5	14.1	14.0	14.8
Less than once a week	4.6	6.7	4.5	4.6
Whenever they appear	3.0	3.7	4.2	4.3
(MEDIUM total)	21.1	24.5	22.7	23.7
LOW				
Not very often	6.8	7.8	12.3	10.5
Hardly at all	7.2	2.6	9.0	8.6
(LOW total)	14.0	10.4	21.3	19.1
Don't know	.8	.4	.6	.9

[5] The question asked was: "During a political campaign you can learn about the campaign in many ways. First, during the last election campaign, how often did you read stories about the political campaign in the newspapers?"

The survey also found that Republicans read more political campaign stories in magazines than did the ticket-splitters and Democrats, with the Democrats again coming in third. But almost half of the electorate paid very little attention to political stories in magazines.

TABLE 16

NATIONAL VOTER INTEREST IN CAMPAIGN STORIES
IN MAGAZINES: 1967[6]
(N = 1169)

Read Campaign Magazine Stories		National Voting Behavior			
		Republican	Ticket-splitter	Democrat	Total
HIGH	Every day without fail	5.5%	1.9%	2.0%	2.4%
		⎱ 10.1	⎱ 7.8	⎱ 7.6	⎱ 7.8
	Almost every day	4.6	5.9	5.6	5.4
MEDIUM	Once or twice a week	25.7	24.2	21.3	20.7
	Less than once a week	13.9 ⎰ 51.8	12.3 ⎰ 51.6	10.1 ⎰ 45.7	11.2 ⎰ 46.1
	Whenever they appear	12.2	15.1	14.3	14.2
LOW	Not very often	19.4	25.7	22.7	23.0
		⎱ 35.9	⎱ 40.6	⎱ 45.1	⎱ 44.6
	Hardly at all	16.5	14.9	22.4	21.6
	Don't know	2.3	—	1.6	1.5

[6] Market Opinion Research, July 1967.

From 1928 until about 1952 radio dominated campaign communications. Since 1952, television has taken over and political advertising on radio has decreased as a proportion of campaign expenses. Recently, however, radio addresses, advertising, and political talk shows have been on the

TABLE 17

NATIONAL VOTER INTEREST AND AUDIENCE FOR POLITICAL TALKS OR SHOWS ON RADIO: 1967[7]

(N = 1169)

Heard Political Talks or Shows		National Voting Behavior			
		Republican	Ticket-splitter	Democrat	Total
HIGH	Every day without fail	9.7%	7.8%	7.8%	8.1%
	Almost every day	12.2	8.2	10.1	9.8
		21.9	16.0	17.9	17.9
MEDIUM	Once or twice a week	8.0	5.9	9.5	7.4
	Less than once a week	5.5	7.4	5.9	5.7
	Whenever they appear	9.7	5.6	10.4	8.6
		23.2	18.9	25.8	21.7
LOW	Not very often	21.5	26.8	24.4	23.6
	Hardly at all	31.2	36.8	30.5	34.4
		52.7	63.6	54.9	58.0
	Don't know	2.2	1.5	1.4	2.4

[7] Market Opinion Research, July 1967.

increase. Today behavioral Republicans use radio as a medium of political information more than do Democrats or ticket-splitters. Fifty-eight percent of the sample said they rarely listened to political talks or shows, and the lowest amount of radio use was among ticket-splitters at 64% (Table 17).

TABLE 18

NATIONAL VOTER INTEREST AND AUDIENCE FOR POLITICAL TALKS OR SHOWS ON TELEVISION: 1967[8]

(N = 1169)

Viewed Political Talks or Shows		National Voting Behavior							
		Republican		Ticket-splitter		Democrat		Total	
HIGH	Every day without fail	20.7%	38.8	15.6%	35.7	12.0%	33.6	15.1%	34.0
	Almost every day	18.1		20.1		21.6		18.9	
MEDIUM	Once or twice a week	15.2	45.2	15.6	48.4	14.8	42.8	15.3	44.1
	Less than once a week	5.9		8.6		9.0		7.6	
	Whenever they appear	24.1		24.2		19.0		21.2	
LOW	Not very often	8.9	15.2	10.0	14.8	14.8	22.7	12.4	20.6
	Hardly at all	6.3		4.8		7.9		8.2	
	Don't know	.8		1.1		.9		1.3	

[8] Market Opinion Research, July 1967.

Let us next consider the use and impact of television, considered by those expert and inexpert in campaign matters to be the most effective medium in political campaigns.

Behavioral Republicans use television as a news medium slightly more than ticket-splitters and Democrats. About 35% of the electorate said they watched it daily and about 45% viewed television on a weekly basis (Table 18).

The tables for voter interest in newspaper, magazine, radio, and television coverage of campaigns are summarized in the following table, which combines the eight categories used earlier into three—daily, weekly, and almost no interest:

TABLE 19

SUMMARY OF NATIONAL VOTER INTEREST AND AUDIENCE
FOR NEWSPAPER, MAGAZINE, RADIO AND TELEVISION
COVERAGE OF CAMPAIGNS: 1967[9]
(N = 1169)

News Media: Audience and Interest	National Voting Behavior			
	Republican	Ticket-splitter	Democrat	Total
Newspapers: Interest and Readership				
Daily	64.1%	64.7%	55.4%	56.3%
Weekly	21.1	24.5	22.7	23.7
Almost none	14.0	10.4	21.3	19.1
Television: Interest and Audience				
Daily	38.8	35.7	33.6	34.0
Weekly	45.2	48.4	42.8	44.1
Almost none	15.2	14.8	22.7	20.6
Radio: Interest and Audience				
Daily	21.9	16.0	17.9	17.9
Weekly	23.2	18.9	25.8	21.7
Almost none	52.7	63.6	54.9	58.0
Magazines: Interest and Readership				
Daily	10.1	7.8	7.6	7.8
Weekly	51.8	51.9	45.7	46.1
Almost none	35.9	40.6	45.1	44.6

[9] The percentages in these categories do not total 100% because the "don't know" responses were not included.

Among those Americans who voted, the majority had a daily and weekly interest in political news as reported by newspapers and television. Voting groups varied in their use of the media. Republicans were heavier users of television, radio, and magazines. Ticket-splitters and Republicans had almost the same degree of interest in newspapers. With the exception of radio, Democrats used the news media less than the other two groups (Table 19).

TABLE 20

INCIDENCE OF PERSONAL CONVERSATIONS
ABOUT CANDIDATES DURING THE LAST MONTH
OF THE CAMPAIGN[10]
(N = 1169)

Incidence of Conversations	National Voting Behavior			
	Republican	Ticket-splitter	Democrat	Total
Several times a week	39.7% ⎤ 71.8	38.4% ⎤ 72.2	31.9% ⎤ 54.6	33.4% ⎤ 60.6
Once or twice a week	32.1 ⎦	33.8 ⎦	22.7 ⎦	27.2 ⎦
Once or twice a month	8.9 ⎤ 28.2	10.0 ⎤ 26.7	18.2 ⎤ 43.7	12.8 ⎤ 37.8
Less often	19.3 ⎦	16.7 ⎦	25.5 ⎦	25.0 ⎦
Don't know	—	1.1	1.7	1.6

10 The question asked was: "Let's go back again to the last political campaign. . . during the last *month* of the campaign, about how often did you have conversations with people about political candidates? Was it: several times a week? Once or twice a week? Once or twice a month? Less often? Market Opinion Research, July 1967.

The traditional literature and folklore of political science tells us that the political independent is less interested in politics and therefore, of course, talks about it less with his neighbors and friends than do the Republican and Democratic partisans.

In weekly conversations about the candidates during the last month before the election, our national ticket-splitters and behavioral Republicans were active at the 72% level and the Democrats trailed at some distance at 54% (Table 20).

TABLE 21

OPINION SOLICITATION BY OTHERS FOR ALL
VOTERS DURING LAST MONTH OF CAMPAIGN[11]
(N = 1169)

Political Opinions Asked:	National Voting Behavior			
	Republican	Ticket-splitter	Democrat	Total
Several times a week	20.7% ⎤ 51.9	26.0% ⎤ 53.9	20.7% ⎤ 43.1	21.1% ⎤ 45.4
Once or twice a week	31.2 ⎦	27.9 ⎦	22.4 ⎦	24.3 ⎦
Once or twice a month	19.0 ⎤ 47.7	17.5 ⎤ 46.1	16.5 ⎤ 56.0	15.6 ⎤ 53.4
Less often	28.7 ⎦	28.6 ⎦	39.5 ⎦	37.8 ⎦
Don't know	.4	—	.9	1.2

11 The question asked was: "During the last month of the campaign (Oct. 1966), about how often would you say people asked for your opinion on politics? Was it . . . Several times a week? Once or twice a week? Once or twice a month? Less often?" Market Opinion Research, July 1967.

OTHER MEDIA INPUTS

The respondents were also questioned about how often people asked their opinions about politics during the month preceding the election:

A majority of ticket-splitters (54%) and Republicans (52%) stated that others had asked their opinions on political matters during the last month of the campaign. Democrats were about 10 points behind at the 43% level. Ticket-splitters (26%) recalled significantly more weekly activity than the other two groups (Table 21).

What role did the ticket-splitter play in the discussion of politics—was he leader or follower?

TABLE 22

LEADERSHIP ROLE PLAYED IN THE
DISCUSSION OF POLITICS[12]
(N = 1169)

Discussion Role	National Voting Behavior			
	Repub-lican	Ticket-splitter	Demo-crat	Total
Mainly listen	42.6%	47.6%	54.3%	50.0%
Try to convince them	15.2	12.6	12.3	12.3
Both	36.3	36.4	27.2	31.6
Don't know	5.9	3.4	6.2	6.1
	100.0	100.0	100.0	100.0

Behavioral Republicans were a bit more activist than other voters in trying to persuade people to their political point of view. Ticket-splitters were a few points behind the Republicans. Both of these groups were more active in the techniques of personal political persuasion than were Democrats.

[12] The question asked was: "When you and your friends discuss politics, what part do you play? Do you mainly listen . . . or do you try to convince them of your ideas?" Market Opinion Research, July 1967.

To summarize, ticket-splitters and Republicans played much more active roles in political opinion formation, discussion, and persuasion than did behavioral Democrats.

It is also supposed that behavioral Republicans and Democrats are much more interested and involved in partisan campaign activity. By traditional definition, independents and ticket-splitters should be disinterested in the rituals of campaigning. Are they?

TABLE 23

CONTACTS WITH REPUBLICAN AND DEMOCRATIC PARTY WORKERS DURING THE CAMPAIGN[13]
(N = 1169)

	National Voting Behavior			
	Repub- lican	Ticket- splitter	Demo- crat	Total
Talked to Democratic Workers				
Yes—Talked with them	80.2%	70.6%	67.5%	75.0%
No—Did not talk with them	19.8	29.4	32.5	25.0
	100.0	100.0	100.0	100.0
Talked to Republican Workers				
Yes—Talked with them	57.4	71.0	84.6	76.3
No—Did not talk with them	42.6	29.0	15.4	23.7
	100.0	100.0	100.0	100.0

Ticket-splitters talked with Republican and Democratic workers in equal proportions—about 71%. Democrats talked to their own partisans more often than did Republicans (67.5 to 57.4%).

We measured direct involvement by the respondents or their spouses in campaigns:

[13]The question asked was: "Did you talk to any party workers, either Democrats or Republicans, during the last election campaign? If yes, which?" Market Opinion Research, July 1967.

TABLE 24

INVOLVEMENT IN POLITICAL CAMPAIGNS[14]

(N = 1169)

Respondent's Campaign Involvement	National Voting Behavior			
	Repub-lican	Ticket-splitter	Demo-crat	Total
Yes/Self only	4.2%	3.3%	2.5%	2.7%
Yes/Spouse only	2.5	.7	.8	1.2
Yes/Both of us	4.6	4.1	3.1	2.9
No/Neither of us	88.7	91.9	93.6	93.2
	100.0	100.0	100.0	100.0

Republicans were the most active campaigners with 11.3% involved. Ticket-splitters were next at 8.1%, followed by Democrats at 6.4%.

Do the campaign activity and other political interests translate into participation in most elections?

TABLE 25

VOTING HABITS OF REPUBLICANS, TICKET-SPLITTERS, AND DEMOCRATS IN THE NATION[15]

(N = 1169)

Voting Habits	National Voting Behavior							
	Total		Republican		Ticket-splitter		Democrat	
Vote in less than half	24.0	10.3%	14.0	3.0%	11.9	3.3%	16.5	5.3%
Vote in about half		13.7		11.0		8.6		11.2
Vote in nearly every election	74.4	36.0	86.0	35.4	88.1	39.8	82.7	38.7
Vote in all elections		38.4		50.6		48.3		44.0
Don't know	1.6		—		—		.8	

[14] The question asked was: "Were you or your husband (wife) actively involved in the campaigning in any way?" Market Opinion Research, July 1967.

[15] The question asked was: "Thinking back about all kinds of

The highest level of regular participation in elections was recorded by ticket-splitters (88.1%) and Republicans (86%), and behavioral Democrats trailed both groups at 82.7%.

Whether family political background might be related to the respondent's voting behavior was another informational input that was tested. The correlations are not as precise as some in other studies would have us believe.

TABLE 26

VOTER'S BEHAVIOR COMPARED WITH
THAT OF HIS FATHER[16]
(N = 1169)

| How Father Voted | National Respondent's Voting Behavior | | | |
	Repub-lican	Ticket-splitter	Demo-cratic	Total
Republican	58.8%	21.9%	13.4%	26.8%
Democrat	19.3	42.8	64.1	44.3
Ticket-splitter	10.1	19.3	6.2	11.5
Other	1.7	3.3	3.6	3.1
Don't know	10.1	12.7	12.7	14.3
	100.0	100.0	100.0	100.0

Ticket-splitting fathers were twice as likely to produce offspring who also split their ballots, and they were twice as likely to produce behavioral Republicans rather than behavioral Democrats. Ticket-splitters came primarily from behavioral Democratic backgrounds (42.8%), and 21.9% came from behavioral Republican backgrounds. Behavioral Democrats (64.1%) were more successful in passing on

elections, such as local school elections, primary elections and general elections, would you say that you vote in less than half of the elections, vote in about one half of all elections, vote in nearly every election, or vote in all elections?" Market Opinion Research, July 1967.

[16] The question asked was: "How would you say your father voted most of the time?" Market Opinion Research, July 1967.

their political faith than were behavioral Republicans
(58.8%).

SUMMARY

With the decrease in straight party voting and the increase in ticket-splitting, we have the following order of
inputs into the decision-making process of the voters:
candidates, issues, party identification, and group affiliations.

Two-thirds of the variables now cited as most important
by voters in their decision-making relate to candidates and
not to the images of the political parties.

Contacts with candidates, talks with political workers,
political brochures, newspaper advertisements, television
advertisements, political mailings, magazine advertisements, billboards, and telephone campaign messages are
nine media variables that can be directly controlled or in
some way manipulated by the campaign. They can be
controlled in the sense that they can be purchased or that
the energies of the candidate can be focused on them.
Eleven of the twelve "very important" variables are not
controllable by the campaign strategists. In the "very important" column, the only one that can be controlled is
"contact with candidates." There are no advertisements in
this "very important" group.

Ticket-splitters and Republicans were found to be
heavier media (newspapers, magazines, radio, and television) users than Democrats. Ticket-splitters and Republicans played much more active roles in political opinion
formulation, discussion, and persuasion than did Democrats.

CHAPTER 5

Campaign Strategies and the Ticket-splitter

*For the electorate as a whole, party is the most powerful
predictor of voting behavior. However, this information is not
very useful to a politician in the middle of a close campaign. . . . Furthermore, there are approximately the same
number of entrenched partisan voters for each of the two
major parties, and their votes largely cancel each other out.
The politician relies on issues, events, circumstances, and strategies to create an image which captures the "crucial minority" of votes that decide the election (or prevents their
being captured by an opposing party). In terms of public
policy, the victorious politician must concern himself with
winning the votes of this crucial minority as well as retaining
the loyalty of those already in his coalition.*

Peter B. Natchez, "Images of Voting,"
Public Policy, Summer 1970

The ticket-splitter did not emerge from our data as a
one-issue person or as a voter who could be easily reached
by highly emotional appeals. Rather he emerged as a
complex voter who had a ready grasp of the campaign
issues and who was oriented toward problem-solving by
candidates rather than by political parties. In competitive
situations, the successful campaign strategies in the 1960's
were those that understood the ticket-splitting phenomenon and therefore understood the ticket-splitters.

We have tried to demonstrate that the candidate who
employs the strategy that best communicates with the
ticket-splitter has the best chance of winning his campaign.

The trends that have recently manifested themselves include the increased importance of the voter's perception of the candidates and their ability to handle problems, the increased reliance by ticket-splitters on certain media, and the unpredictability of the American voter despite sophisticated measuring techniques. Understanding election outcomes and their effects on public policy has become much more difficult than in the past. In many states or Congressional districts that once automatically voted Democratic or Republican, it is no longer possible to predict voting behavior on the basis of party identification. It is also no longer possible to predict voting behavior on the basis of socio-economic status or positions on certain issues.[1]

The way voters see and use media is becoming one of the most significant factors in the way people make up their minds about candidates. The way to win elections is not through traditional television advertising that "sells" the candidate, but through an overall communications strategy linking the candidate and the target groups which constitute the "crucial minority" that will decide the election. The model on pages 93-94 was constructed in attempting to reach ticket-splitters. A campaign is seen as a set of subsystems. Two of the systems (voting behavior and demographics) supply information to the candidate about how people have voted in the past. The other two subsystems (media data and opinion polling) are part of a "loop" information system monitoring changes in media use and attitudes about politics and voting intentions. The last subsystem provides information for routine organizational activities. The data that flow from these five subsystems are the chief ingredients in the development of an overall campaign strategy to influence ticket-splitters.

Emphasis in this model is on the contemporary; we are concerned about how people use media today and how they feel about the candidates and issues right now. The key to successful campaigning is the maintenance of a two-way communications system in which the information in either direction is ideally never more than a few hours

[1] See "A New Political Realignment?" by Everett Ladd, Jr., Charles Hadley, and Lauriston King, *The Public Interest*, Spring 1971.

old. While past behavior and demographic characteristics give points of reference, they are not the critical variables in explaining and predicting the behavior of ticket-splitters.

Many statewide campaigns in this country have already been run on the basis of the concepts contained in this model. The first to use the model was the 1962 Michigan gubernatorial campaign. We shall examine that campaign in some detail and shall also examine the most recent, and much revised, application of this campaign model in the 1970 Michigan gubernatorial election.

CAMPAIGN INFORMATION SYSTEM FOR TICKET-SPLITTER STRATEGY

Subsystem 1: Voting Behavior
Analyses of past voting behavior from smallest possible political units.

Detection of trends.

Many levels of analysis to find straight party voting, ticket-splitting, turnout.

Subsystem 2: Demographics
Best predictors: income, age, education, occupation, race and residence.

Subsystem 3: Media Markets
Media use by voting behavior.

Media use by demographics.

Media important in political decision-making.

Subsystem 4: Opinion Polling
Identify Republicans, Democrats, and Ticket-splitters. Construct profiles based on: demographics, attitudes on candidates, issues and parties, media use.

Isolate variables important to campaign decisions.

SUMMARY OF DATA FROM INFORMATION FLOW

Relationships of the data in the systems.

Selection of variables most important to the campaign.

Outline the implications for campaign strategies.

Subsystem 5:   Organizational Activities
    Collection and computerization
    of name files, mobilization of
    support, fund raising, mail
    campaigns, voter activities.

THE CAMPAIGN PLAN

    Target groups: undecideds,
    ticket-splitters.

    Resource allocation: time,
    media, organizational and
    other activities.

    Relate vital information from
    the demographic, media and
    polling subsystems to target
    groups.

    Pretest campaign techniques
    and media appeals.

    Draw organization plans.

    Prepare research on issues.

    Adopt media schedule.

    Adopt budget.

    Prepare decision flow chart.

BEGIN CAMPAIGN

THE FIRST TICKET-SPLITTER STRATEGY

In the early spring of 1962 when George Romney of Michigan began discussing and planning the strategy for that year's gubernatorial campaign, his political strategists drew upon the findings of the Survey Research Center on partisans and independents, and also from Murray Levin's work on voter alienation.[2] At the outset of that campaign

[2] For a more detailed and colorful account of the ticket-splitter

it was the intention of the strategists to identify, physically locate, and then make campaign targets of those voters who thought of themselves as "independents." Secondly, the proposed strategy was to seek out those who were most alienated from government—the state government in particular—and convince them to do something about their alienation by splitting their ballots for Republican George Romney.

Michigan voters perceived themselves in terms of party identification at that time as follows: 42.3% as Democrats, 29.9% as Republicans, and 26.6% as independents; 1.2% did not state their attitudes.[3] To win meant that the Republican gubernatorial candidate would have to take all of the Republican identifiers, more than two-thirds of the independents, and a share of the Democrats as well. This opinion research appeared to present Romney with an almost overwhelming campaign task. When the campaign began in the summer of 1962, the undecided voters in the gubernatorial contest were basically Democratic, urban, and middle or lower middle class. When the behavioral definition was used, 40.5% said they voted Democratic, 23.7% said they voted Republican (down 6% over the identifiers), and 35.7% were ticket-splitters (up almost 10% over those who identified as independents). The target group of independents grew by about 10% when the behavioral definition was used!

The ticket-splitters consisted of Democrats in the Detroit metropolitan area and Republicans in outstate Michigan. At the time of the first poll, the Romney campaign staff also conducted a precinct-by-precinct analysis of the Detroit area. It showed that the areas of higher ticket-splitting were centered in precincts of high Democratic support. By subtracting the average Republican vote from the vote for the 1960 Republican gubernatorial candidate, a voter deviation percentage was determined for the pre-

technique and strategy of the Romney campaigns, see T. George Harris, *Romney's Way: A Man and An Idea* (Englewood Cliffs: Prentice-Hall, 1967), Chapter 16.

[3] In the years since then, these Michigan percentages have remained about the same in statewide polls conducted by Market Opinion Research. They are remarkably similar to the national identifications as measured by Gallup during 1971.

cinct—that is, the number and percentage of ticket-splitters.

Voter turnout, 1960 census information, and other political data were collected to form a profile of forty-seven
"market areas" in Wayne County. These market areas had
homogeneous socio-economic characteristics, natural
boundaries, ethnic and religious similarities, certain shop-
ping patterns and traffic flow, and similar political behavior. The areas were then rank ordered from high to low
incidence of ticket-splitting and voter turnout.[4] From the
demographic information in their polls and the census
tract data, which were overlaid on the precinct voting
statistics, the Romney campaign staff constructed profiles
of the 1962 committed and uncommitted gubernatorial
voters. Then the social and political differences between
ticket-splitters and self-defined independents became most
clear. The ticket-splitter's profile turned out to be this:
owner of a modest home (about $15,000), white-collar or
a highly skilled industrial worker, earned over $7,000 in
income, and slightly more Catholic than Protestant. Match-
ing this information with the census tract data and voting
behavior research, it was possible to physically locate the
small areas which contained high proportions of ticket-
splitters. The surveys also revealed that most of the political characteristics attributed to independents by the Survey Research Center did not apply to these ticket-splitters.

In 1962, ticket-splitters were the heaviest users of media
of all three groups. Like the other voters, they preferred
newspapers over television:

[4] Also rank ordered were the political areas of the state in terms
of their contribution to the vote totals. This we named the *contribution-ratio* statistical technique, which determines the percentage a
given political unit (i.e., precinct, ward, city, township, or county)
contributes to the total state vote and to a candidate's total in the
gubernatorial contest. Obviously it is important to know where the
votes are—both in terms of numbers and physical location. The
contribution-ratio analysis can be one variable in determining the
amount of the candidate's time, advertising, and other resources to
be expended in the various cities and counties of the state. In
Michigan nineteen out of the eighty-three counties contribute 81%
of the total vote in the gubernatorial race. The Romney campaign
efforts were directed at these nineteen heavyweight counties, and,
within these counties, to the city, precinct, and township levels.

MEDIA USE: REPUBLICANS, DEMOCRATS, AND TICKET-
SPLITTERS IN 1962 MICHIGAN GUBERNATORIAL CAMPAIGN[5]
(N = 600)

Voting Groups	Media Activity Yesterday		
	Newspapers	Television	Radio
Republicans	72.9%	62.8%	51.6%
Democrats	66.5	66.1	51.3
Ticket-splitters	77.2	75.6	62.2

A similar after-election study conducted in December of 1966 revealed that Republicans and ticket-splitters were more active readers of political stories in news columns and political advertising than were the Democrats:

DAILY POLITICAL READING BY VOTING GROUPS[6]
(N = 800)

Reading Newspapers Every Day	Voting Groups		
	Repub- licans	Ticket- splitters	Demo- crats
News columns	69.8%	69.4%	58.9%
Political ads	62.6	57.1	45.9

Ticket-splitters paid as much attention to news columns as did the Republicans and gave almost as much attention to political advertising. This suggests that they had a good deal of interest in political news and other information events.

A 1962 post-election study also confirmed that ticket-splitters were involved in campaign activity: 7.9% of the ticket-splitters said they had been involved in the campaign

[5] Market Opinion Research, December 1962.
[6] Market Opinion Research, December 1966.

as compared with 6.7% for the Democrats and 10.6% for
the Republicans. They also had a significant number of
contacts with party workers of both sides—39.5% as a-
gainst 29.3% for Republicans and 26.8% for the Democrats. The Michigan Republican Party workers in 1962 did
a better job of contacting the ticket-splitters than did the
Democrats:

PARTY WORKER CONTACTS WITH REPUBLICANS,
DEMOCRATS AND TICKET-SPLITTERS, 1962 ELECTION[7]
(N = 600)

Voting Groups	Party Workers	
	Republicans	Democrats
Republicans	85.5%	34.5%
Democrats	56.9	72.2
Ticket-splitters	78.0	64.0

Ticket-splitters had received more campaign literature at
74.8% than Democrats at 60.6% and Republicans at
60.6%. And they had received more literature from the
Republicans than from the Democrats.

Ticket-splitters had also talked with more union political workers and had read a good deal about the campaign
in union newspapers.

All three groups showed a relatively high degree of
personal contact with the two gubernatorial candidates,
with ticket-splitters leading at 15.7% followed by Democrats at 11.5% and Republicans at 10.6%. Of those who
had met one or both of the candidates, the contacts were
as follows:

[7] Market Opinion Research, December 1962.

VOTERS MEETING GUBERNATORIAL CANDIDATES, 1962 ELECTION[8]
(N = 600)

	Percent Meeting Candidates	
Voting Groups	Romney	Swainson
Republicans	80.0%	40.0%
Democrats	35.5	87.0
Ticket-splitters	95.0	50.0
All voters	64.9	64.9

George Romney was extremely successful in contacting the ticket-splitters; he contacted nearly twice as many of these key voters as did his opponent.

The data implies that ticket-splitters meet more candidates than do behavioral Republicans and Democrats. If ten ticket-splitters who said they had met a candidate were to get together, odds are that five of them would have met both of the candidates.

In the 1962 Romney gubernatorial campaign a "ticket-splitter" was defined as one who deviated from his traditional party behavior at the Presidential or gubernatorial level. At the state level, a "ticket-splitter" was anyone who voted a straight party ticket for the administrative board candidate (e.g., secretary of state, attorney general) and the local candidates, but who split off in the vote for governor and/or President.[9] In Michigan the vote for state attorney general was used as the index of straight party

[8] Market Opinion Research, December 1962.

[9] Ticket-splitting at the precinct level is computed by comparing the attorney general candidate's percentage of the vote in that race with the gubernatorial candidate's percentage in his race. For example, if the Republican candidate for attorney general received 40% of a precinct's vote and the gubernatorial candidate garnered 48%, this represents a rather high deviation of 8%. In Michigan, the differences run from 0% in many rural precincts and some small cities to a high of 10% in the suburbs of the Detroit metropolitan area.

voting. In general, the closer to the three-county Detroit metropolitan area, the higher was the incidence of ticket-splitting. In Detroit itself, ticket-splitting was highest on the outskirts of the city and decreased toward the core city. While ticket-splitting is characteristic of the Detroit metropolitan area, it is not true of all other large cities in Michigan.[10]

The 1962 gubernatorial campaign—probably the most research-oriented of any statewide campaign for Republicans up to that point—demonstrated the utility of the ticket-splitter concept. George Romney won that close race with 51.4% of the vote. This achievement can be explained only by a communications strategy directed toward ticket-splitters.

These findings with respect to the Michigan ticket-splitter were applied to voters in other states. Continued research by other campaign consultants, including Market Opinion Research, The Communications Company, Ed Nichols and Associates, and the firm of Bailey, Deardourff, and Bowen, has only supported the findings in Michigan and their implications for the building of campaign communications strategies. Lance Tarrance later applied the concept to resource allocation in Texas campaigns, particularly in the area of the candidate's time in selected counties, neighborhoods, and precincts.[11]

The elections of the 1970's will be shaped by the attitudes and actions of the ticket-splitters in America. The most recent Michigan gubernatorial campaign, which was in many ways based on the ticket-splitter strategy of 1962, is, we believe, a harbinger of many campaigns in this decade. The political profile of Michigan—both in terms of voters who identify as Republicans, Democrats, and inde-

---

[10] It should be noted that these findings do not square with those of Campbell and Miller as reported in "The Motivational Basis of Straight and Split-Ticket Voting," *American Political Science Review*, June 1957. On the basis of the research they conducted in 1956, Campbell and Miller concluded that "splitting at the state and local level is much less common in metropolitan areas than it is outside these areas" (pp. 296-297).

[11] A seminar on ticket splitting was held in Pittsburgh in March of 1970. Some of the researchers cited above created a technical manual on the major findings from past campaigns. This manual will soon be published jointly by Market Opinion Research, Inc. and Politicon, Inc.

pendents and in terms of those who behave as Republicans, Democrats, and ticket-splitters—is almost identical to the national profile. Thus we believe it is reasonable to generalize from the 1970 campaign for governor in Michigan and look ahead to the Presidential and statewide campaigns of 1972 and beyond.

TICKET-SPLITTER CAMPAIGN STRATEGY IN 1970

Governor William Milliken was one of only two Midwestern Republican governors who won in 1970. He received 50.7% of the vote. In most Michigan statewide races (e.g., U. S. Senator, secretary of state, attorney general) the average Republican vote was only slightly over 40%.

There were three constitutional amendments on the 1970 Michigan ballot. The first dealt with a $100 million low-income housing bond issue, which the governor strongly supported. It lost, 60-40. The second proposal on the ballot was the eighteen-year-old vote, which was also strongly endorsed by the governor. It lost, 60-40. The third—and highly controversial—proposal prohibited aid to non-public schools. The governor opposed the passage of that amendment and it carried about 60-40. In short, the vote on the rest of the statewide ballot for Republicans ran against Governor Milliken by about 60-40. He won, against these odds, primarily by designing his campaign to communicate with ticket-splitters in Michigan.

In the 1970 national electorate as a whole, Milliken's victory was also against the odds. Democrats in 1970 took thirteen governorships away from the Republicans—registering the most impressive net gain in state houses of any party since 1938. The total gubernatorial vote across the country in 1970 showed a Democratic plurality of over one million votes.[12]

Campaign planning began in February of 1970 with a precinct-by-precinct analysis throughout the entire state of the 1966 gubernatorial election. This computerized analysis revealed the location of those precincts with the heaviest amount of ticket-splitting (i.e., the difference between the vote for Governor Romney and the Republican

[12] See "1970 Voting Patterns: Widespread Ticket-Splitting," *Congressional Quarterly*, July 2, 1971.

candidate for attorney general). These precincts were then ordered—from highest to lowest—in terms of amount of ticket-splitting in them. Voter turnout data were added to the mix. Because nineteen of Michigan's eighty-three counties contribute more than 80% of the vote, these nineteen "heavyweight" counties—with the precincts within them rank ordered by the amount of ticket-splitting—became the principal target in the allocation of campaign resources. The greater the amount of ticket-splitting, the greater the allocation of the candidate's time, the greater the media exposure, and the greater the organizational effort.

The political profile of the state—remarkably similar to Michigan in 1962 and the national profile in 1970—looked like this:

	Self-Identification	Voting Behavior	
Republican	30%	Straight Republican	25%
Democrat	45	Straight Democrat	40
Independent	25	Ticket-splitter	35

Again there was a discrepancy between those who identified as independents and those who actually split their ballots. Governor Milliken could win, it was determined, if he captured all of the behavioral Republican voters, 75% of the ticket-splitters, and about 10% of the behavioral Democrats. The target group was the ticket-splitters, who also comprised the bulk of the undecided gubernatorial voters in the first in-depth poll, conducted in May 1970. Throughout the entire campaign, all of the characteristics of the gubernatorial undecideds and the ticket-splitters remained the same.

In the published polls of the *Detroit News* and in the private polls, the governor never exceeded 48% of the vote, from May through election day. The undecided vote among the ticket-splitters remained unusually high throughout the campaign. This was common in many of the 1970 campaigns and probably means that elections in the 1970's will be characterized by high amounts of indecision among ticket-splitters right up to election day.

Governor Milliken's approval rating (of the way he handled his job) was a high 65% at first and then dropped very slightly to about 60% throughout the rest of the campaign. Seventy-three per cent of the behavioral Republicans approved of the way he was handling his job, 50% of the behavioral Democrats, and 68% of the ticket-splitters. Among the gubernatorial undecideds, 50% approved of his performance. Most of those who approved said they felt strongly about their answer. The campaign challenge was how to move the ticket-splitters who approved of the way the governor was handling his job to a voting commitment for him.

The first in-depth poll revealed that the ticket-splitters knew very little about the governor, either as a personality or as someone related to specific state problems or accomplishments. There were practically no negative attitudes about him. In short, most Michigan ticket-splitters knew he was governor and approved of what he was doing as governor, but were unable to say why. The overall campaign plan, therefore, contained a communications strategy aimed at ticket-splitters which would provide them with information about the governor, his accomplishments, the way he was handling the state problems, and his future goals.

Emphasis was on providing information—not propaganda. The campaign strategists constantly focused on those media and techniques that would best communicate accurate information about Governor Milliken to ticket-splitters. The information stressed Milliken as governor, stressed his incumbency and experience, and reiterated the theme that the governor had a record of understanding problems and was doing things to solve them. The emphasis was put on his *ability to handle problems* and his *ability to handle the job* of governor. He did not promise to solve all the state's problems; he promised to do a better job than his opponent. Our research revealed that the ticket-splitters had a higher level of alienation and distrust of politicians than behavioral Republicans and Democrats. Utopian promises in policy statements and advertisements would tend to have a negative effect, and candidates who followed this course would not be believed by the ticket-splitters. This alienation had been increasing during the 1960's and should continue in the 1970's.

The communications program also stressed the governor's personal characteristics, always in the role of governor. His competence, integrity, and dynamism were emphasized by pointing to the way he handled the state's problems. The people approved of the way he handled his job, and all of the campaign communications reinforced that perception.

Campaigns are commonly thought to need a principal "theme." The Milliken campaign was no different, and it had two themes. The first, developed by an advertising agency, was: "The Governor's Office is No Place for Beginners." After running a series of newspaper ads, the campaign strategists conducted a pre-test of this theme, along with some others, among ticket-splitters. It was found that because Milliken had been in office only eighteen months, many ticket-splitters viewed *him* as the beginner. What was supposed to have been a powerful campaign theme was found to be working *against* the candidate. It was replaced with a much more prosaic—but successfully pre-tested—theme: "A Leader You Can Trust."

Instead of the traditional Labor Day to election day campaign, the campaign staff and the staff of the Executive Office were directed to think of the period from May 15 through November 3 as a period of increased communications between the governor and the voters—particularly the ticket-splitter. The governor had to make news and be in the news.

In Chapter IV we stated that we found the most important factor in the voting decision of the ticket-splitter to be news or confrontation formats on television and radio and in the newspapers. Traditional political advertisements ranked as relatively unimportant. Keeping these priorities in mind, the Milliken strategists advised that the campaign be news oriented. Instead of expecting the governor to abandon his duties during the campaign period, as the incumbent usually does, they encouraged him to pay more attention to them, with as much news coverage as possible. The campaign acquired the services of a photographer who shot sound and silent film of the governor's activities on nearly a daily basis. These film clips were made available to the state's television stations. Outside the Detroit metropolitan area, they were used an estimated 60% of the time in daily TV newscasts. The same was done for radio stations with a beeper system. The normal written press releases for newspapers were also produced and distributed.

As part of the "on the job" strategy, Governor Milliken did not make the traditional policy speeches in appropriate locations (for example, a speech before the Detroit Economic Club on taxation). Instead, he presented his position on the major issues in his Lansing capitol office before the state capitol press corps. The Executive Office staff was directed to handle press conferences as principally audiovisual and not print-oriented events.

The controlled, or advertising, phase of this communications program started September 1st on television and radio. The advertisement strategy, too, was based on our research into the ticket-splitter. The Milliken television commercials were created following a "mini-documentary" or "tele-news" concept, to make the commercials look like news. Each of the nine spots opened with a dramatic still photograph representing one of the state's most urgent problems. Most of these stills were in black and white accentuating the graphic starkness of the problem. The scene then dissolved from the still photograph to the governor, who in each of the nine spots was seen as demonstrating his understanding of that particular problem and addressing himself to its solution. These color segments of the governor all contained identifiable symbols of the governor's office—state seal, flag or desk. The commercial ended by dissolving to a card which read: "Milliken: A Leader You Can Trust." An announcer's voice-over editorialized in a soft-sell manner: "Think about that on November 3rd." The format: present the problem, demonstrate an understanding and ability to handle that problem, and end with a soft-sell editorial.

Four of these thirty-second commercials were edited and combined into a wrap-up commercial which displayed the four problems and then cut to a voting machine where the lever over Governor Milliken's name was pressed. This spot was a conscious effort to show the voter how to split his ticket for Milliken, demonstrating visually how it could be done on a voting machine.

Two other spots were developed later in the campaign. They were dubbed by the campaign staff the "warm and human" commercials and portrayed the governor in "what kind of man is he" terms, again within the context of the governor's office.

Most advertising agencies, once commercials are produced, make time buys and then send the spots to the television stations to be aired as the station sees fit on a rotation schedule. The Milliken campaign rejected that procedure. Our research indicated that ticket-splitters tend to watch newscasts and sporting events more than behavioral Republicans and Democrats do. Audience analyses also showed that networks and individual channels have audiences with disparate demographic characteristics. By combining what they knew about the audiences of individual networks and channels with what they knew about the ticket-splitter, the Milliken strategists were able to greatly improve the chances of reaching this target group.

Then too, the random assignment of commercials to programs might have been counter-productive—e.g., a hard-hitting crime commercial in the middle of *Laugh-In*. Thus each television spot was assigned on the basis of specific program adjacencies. Hard-hitting commercials on drugs and crime were placed in or next to newscasts or television shows that had themes of violence (e.g., *Mod Squad, Hawaii 5-0)*. Commercials on education (a particular concern of undecided women voters) were placed in or next to highly rated women's programs.[13]

To further assure that audiences with certain ticket-splitter characteristics were being reached, the firm of De Vries and Associates began conducting opinion polls by telephone in weathervane precincts in the state's fourteen media markets.[14] The "media market" concept was added

[13] An October 27 statewide poll revealed that there were more female undecided voters than males. Based on this finding, the campaign strategists decided to buy television time for the last four days of the campaign.

[14] A "weathervane" precinct is one that had the same percentage of the votes for governor as the larger unit of which it was a part (e.g., ward or city).

to the other concepts involved in the ticket-splitting strategy because ticket-splitters do not rely on the political party or their group affiliations for their information on politics and government. They rely on news media. Thus it was no longer sensible to think of the state in terms of the traditional political or governmental units of cities, townships, or counties. Instead, the state was analyzed by areas of media coverage—television and radio stations and newspapers which dominate definable market areas.

Media markets were expected to differ in their concern about issues, in their perceptions of the candidate, and in their voting intentions. And in the almost 6,000 telephone interviews conducted by De Vries and Associates during September and October, these differences were indeed found. The data was put to use in the communications program. For example, air and water pollution was considered an especially pressing state problem in the Kalamazoo and Traverse City media markets, while crime and drugs were considered most important in the Flint and Detroit markets. The assignment of the Milliken spots was related to the rank order of the issues among undecided voters within each of the fourteen media markets. The commercials were adjusted every two weeks during September and October to reflect the changing concerns about the state's problems among the ticket-splitters.

This weekly—almost daily—measurement of the ticket-splitter's concerns about public problems (statewide and local) was a critical variable in the ability of the campaign to communicate with ticket-splitters, both within and outside of the advertising effort. The issue priorities did shift during the last four weeks of the campaign. During the summer and through September, the dominant issue had been what Richard Scammon and Ben Wattenberg called "the social issue" (law and order, crime, drugs, violence, etc.).[15] By the end of September, the concerns of the ticket-splitters started to shift to economic problems (unemployment, the General Motors strike, taxes, state spending, etc.). Had the Milliken campaign not been repeatedly monitoring the concerns of the ticket-splitter, this signifi-

[15] *The Real Majority* (New York: Coward-McCann, Inc., 1970), p. 43.

cant shift would have been missed and the communications efforts of the news media and advertising campaigns would have missed the mark. Other studies conducted in other states in the last weeks of the 1970 campaign indicated the same shift from social to economic concerns.

This telephone polling program—probably the most extensive ever used in a statewide campaign—allowed the campaign staff to monitor constantly the effectiveness of Governor Milliken's total communications effort in reaching the critical target groups. It detected, through panel interviewing, ticket-splitters who had moved from indecision to a commitment for one of the two gubernatorial candidates during the course of the campaign, and why they had moved. And it gave the strategists information about the success of various specific campaign techniques.

On the basis of the findings on radio use, the campaign made a modest radio advertising effort. Radio was viewed as a reinforcing rather than a converting medium. The radio spots were taken from the audio portion of the television commercials. This was done because it was found that radio listeners tend to recall the video part of a television commercial when hearing the audio portion.[16] To provide continuity, the same announcer was used as the voice-over in both the radio and television commercials. On ethnic and black radio, the campaign staff gave the announcers (mostly disc jockeys) some copy and told them to "wing" it. This was done because research findings suggested that blacks and some ethnic groups (recent immigrants) used media that are essentially verbal, i.e., word-of-mouth information received from friends, neighbors, relatives, or from specialized media such as black radio or television. Later in the campaign some radio commercials were produced which used editorial quotes endorsing Governor Milliken. This was an attempt to use one medium (newspapers) to reinforce voters on another medium (radio). The commercials were tailored for individual media markets.

Originally, the campaign plan provided for 1800-line newspaper advertisements that would use the same photograph and word copy that was in the television advertise-

[16] Roper Study.

ments. Six advertisements were planned and one was placed in all of the state's daily newspapers, but the bulk of the program was cancelled. The cancellation occurred because the polling showed that nobody had seen the advertisements and the campaign managers felt the print media money could be put to better use. They decided to produce a rotogravure piece—a Sunday supplement—which would reach every home in Michigan that subscribed to a Sunday newspaper. These 3 million supplements were distributed on the second to last and the last Sunday preceding the election.

Early in the campaign it had been decided to reserve a sizable block of money for a last-minute effort either on television (a thirty-minute documentary) or a rotogravure piece. The decision to go with the rotogravure section rather than the thirty-minute election eve telecast was made in the middle of September when the polling revealed that the Milliken television advertising was not having an effect on the ticket-splitters. The decision then was to go to print media as a way to get information to the ticket-splitters. Subsequent research proved this to be a most timely and appropriate strategy. The rotogravure piece was designed as an information piece—and not an advertising supplement. It was not a hard-sell piece; only on the last page did it ask for a vote for the governor, and in no place did it stress political party. It was designed to be understood visually, so that the reader could get the message without reading the text. Entitled "The Governor," it stressed Milliken's incumbency and his ability to handle the state's problems and ended by pointing out that if the voter approved of the job Governor Milliken was doing, he should vote to keep him in office.

At the beginning of the campaign, personalized direct mail was seen as a significant way to communicate with ticket-splitters. But an experimental study conducted in August among middle- and upper middle-income ticket-splitters found that a robotyped, personal, first-class letter from the governor to each registered voter's home did not significantly shift undecided voters to him. The campaign strategists were not, however, ready to abandon the direct mail communications technique. Another experimental study was conducted, this time among middle- and lower middle-income ticket-splitters who lived in Catholic, blue-collar neighborhoods. This time the personal letter from the governor shifted about 10% of the ticket-splitters from undecided to a commitment. On the basis of this evidence, the campaign staff prepared and mailed some 175,000 computerized direct-mail letters to selected ticket-splitting precincts, principally in the northeast area of the city of Detroit and the Detroit metropolitan area suburbs.

Indecision among the ticket-splitters remained high during the campaign. The weekend preceding the election, the *Detroit News* Poll still showed 5% of the electorate undecided and said that the election was too close to call. An interpretation of these polling results by De Vries and Associates indicated that a high percentage of these voters were ticket-splitters and that there was a slight movement toward Governor Milliken. The last poll, taken on October 29, revealed an extremely close contest with Milliken slightly ahead.

A post-election panel study revealed that those ticket-splitters who decided in the last five days, moved at a ratio of 2 to 1 for Governor Milliken over Sander Levin. It also showed that the registered voters who did not vote would have voted 3-1 for Levin over Milliken. The principal reason given by those who moved from indecision to Milliken was that he had the experience and the ability to do the job. They felt that he could better handle state problems than his opponent.

In short, the campaign strategy to reach ticket-splitters with a communications strategy emphasizing the ability of the governor to perform the job succeeded. It succeeded because the governor—through a good two-way information system—could address himself to the concerns of the Michigan ticket-splitters. It succeeded because the governor had the information to select the media which could best deliver his communications.

SUMMARY

In the Presidential, gubernatorial, and senatorial contests, every state but two (Louisiana and Mississippi) is now competitive. Each of the two major political parties has a chance to win *these* elections if its candidates appeal to the ticket-splitters in that state.

The development of this body of knowledge about ticket-splitters was done by campaign consultants working with Republican candidates in the Midwestern and Eastern states. The Republican Party—in terms of the voters' identification with it—has been a minority party in these states during the 1960's and is apt to remain so during the 1970's. Republican candidates, therefore, will have to continue their efforts to understand and communicate with ticket-splitters. Unlike the Democrats, there are few—if any—states in which Republicans can win statewide elections with just those who identify as Republicans. In most states, Republican candidates need all of the Republican voters and at least half of the ticket-splitters in order to be competitive with Democratic candidates. This situation is particularly acute in Presidential contests, where a Republican candidate in a two-man contest cannot win unless he has all of those who are behavioral Republicans (about 30%) and almost all of those who behave consistently as ticket-splitters (about 35%). Strategically, communicating with and convincing the American ticket-splitter is still—and will continue to be—a major problem for Republican candidates.

Any study of successful Republican Presidential or statewide candidates will reveal that the basis for their victories lay in the implementation of a strategy which communicated the candidate and his views on the issues to large numbers of ticket-splitters. These candidates avoided party appeals—from John Tower in Texas to Nelson Rockefeller in New York.

While reaching the ticket-splitter is the principal strategic problem confronting Republican candidates in the 1970's, Democratic candidates will also have to tailor their campaigns to the concerns and behavior patterns of this increasing group of voters. The decreasing identification of young voters with both political parties along with a growing split-ballot behavior means that both political parties will need to increase their understanding of this phenomenon.

CHAPTER 6

The Ticket-splitter in the 1970's

An appeal based largely on appearing to be "different"— new to politics, or willing to discuss the issues more frankly than usual for candidates, or even frontally attacking re-established party structure—helped produce some of 1970's more notable victories. . . . The search for the non-political newcomer seems sure to intensify. Ticket-splitting has become epidemic. All registration figures and opinion polls show increasing percentages promising to vote "for the man, not the party." The millions of young people now coming on the rolls voice this sentiment even more strongly than their parents. . . .
Alan L. Otten
The *Wall Street Journal*, July 28, 1971

The purpose of this book is to describe and thereby understand a phenomenon which has had a profound effect on American political life during the 1960's. The rapid growth of a large number of voters who regularly split their ballots between the candidates of the Republican and Democratic parties has meant that the traditional two-party analysis of American voting behavior has lost its explanatory power.

We challenge the way academics, pollsters, and other political analysts have traditionally looked at American voters—as self-identified Republicans, Democrats, and independents—because it no longer makes sense to explain them in terms of their self-perceptions—what they think they are. The only way to understand American voters is to examine their behavior—what they actually do. By

113

measuring independence by behavior—splitting the ticket—
we have put together a completely different profile of
those American voters who are the critical element in the
winning or losing of most competitive campaigns at the
state level and the level of the Presidency.

PAST RESEARCH INADEQUATE

Our findings should indicate to political analysts that
the traditional ways to explain and predict voting behavior
are now inadequate. At one time, voting behavior could be
predicted by knowing the political party identification of
the voter and his past voting behavior. If he identified with
the Democratic Party he would likely vote Democratic,
and if he behaved as a Republican in the past he would
behave as a Republican in the future.[1] That is the politics
of the past.

Behavior could also be predicted by knowing the voter's
group affiliations and loyalties. If he were a union member
he would vote straight Democratic, and if he were a
businessman he would vote Republican. Church, business,
professional, and ethnic characteristics were once considered prime determinants of voting behavior. They are
not prime determinants today.[2]

Another method of predicting behavior was to examine
the socio-economic characteristics of the voter. Age, income, occupation, education, race, place of residence, and
other demographics became the predictive variables.[3] The
higher the income, the greater the probability of straight
Republican voting—the reverse being true for Democrats.
Again, recent data on ticket-splitters introduces numerous
exceptions to these kinds of relationships.

One of the first consequences, then, of the emergence of
this large number of ticket-splitters is that political anal-

[1] See *The American Voter*, by Campbell et al. (New York: Wiley,
1960).

[2] See *Voting*, by Berelson et al. (Chicago: U. of Chicago Press,
1954).

[3] See *Political Man: The Social Bases of Politics*, by Seymour
Lipset (Garden City: Doubleday-Anchor, 1960).

ysts are unable to explain voting behavior simply by using the research techniques of the 1940's and 1950's.

During the 1960's, many political strategists found it necessary to use polling more extensively, to get more information on how voters make up their minds about candidates, issues, and parties. Today we especially need information on how a voter sees himself on a liberal/conservative continuum—not just on an ideological basis, but on a variety of specific domestic and foreign policy matters. Because the ticket-splitters are so candidate-oriented, it is also necessary to measure in detail their perceptions of the candidate's ability to do the job, his ability to handle specific public problems, and his stand on important issues.

It was once possible to equate an officeholder's approval/disapproval rating with voting intention. That is, it was assumed that if an undecided voter approved of the job an officeholder was doing, he would be likely to translate that approval into a vote for the candidate when he did decide. Our research suggests that this is no longer so. In the 1970 Michigan gubernatorial election, large numbers of ticket-splitters gave Governor Milliken high and strong approval ratings as governor, but did not vote for him. Those who interpret Gallup and Harris approval/disapproval ratings of President Nixon and other officeholders as indicative of probable voter support are misinterpreting the data.

In short, we are finding that even with all of this knowledge about past voting behavior, group affiliations, demographics, and perceptions of candidates, issues, and parties, we still have only a partial explanation. Many voters—principally the ticket-splitters, who make up a sizable portion of the undecided voters in elections—draw their attitudes about candidates and their positions on issues from the media (principally television) and interpersonal relationships (family and friends). Ticket-splitters do not rely on political parties or their group affiliations—they rely on the news media for their information about politics and government. Most private and public polls do not measure or attempt to understand these inputs.

MORE POLLING RESEARCH

Campaign strategists and other political analysts will have to spend a good deal more money on public-opinion polling during the 1970's. Research on the voters' perceptions, attitudes, media use and other variables related to decision-making will have to become more sophisticated and refined. Candidates will have to devise strategies that will use the right media to set up a two-way communications system with ticket-splitters.

"Nationwide" or "statewide" polls—both by private and public pollsters—will likely have only a limited utility in the 1970's. It is meaningless to have data that tells the campaign strategist: "Americans believe . . . " or "the people of Michigan think. . . ." Polling research must become more localized (by standard metropolitan statistical areas or by media markets) if we are to gain useful information about ticket-splitters.

Furthermore, polling research in the 1970's will have to be conducted more rapidly than in the past. Overnight intelligence on the effectiveness of the candidate's communications efforts and the campaign techniques will become regular features of a successful campaign plan. Information will eventually have to be available to a candidate on a short-time basis.

Then too, polling will have to become more specialized as it becomes more and more difficult to reach target groups of ticket-splitters. The rapid proliferation of special-audience radio stations together with the spread of cable television will challenge the medium of standard television during the 1970's. Measuring the impact of these media on voters can only increase the complexity of the situation.

Research will be more experimental in nature as it becomes increasingly necessary to test communications and media techniques constantly for their effectiveness in influencing voters. More testing of campaign themes, film and video tape commercials, direct mail, and other attempts to communicate will be inevitable.

Polling will have to be done at a much higher frequency than in the past. The 1970's will see more competitive races than the sixties. As the number of ticket-splitters increases, the number of undecided voters will increase. The increased reliance on media for information in the candidate decision-making process will probably be reflected by more voters remaining undecided for longer periods of time. This, of course, will increase the measurement problem and will make voting behavior even more difficult to understand and predict.

In sum, communications strategies for ticket-splitters will need more research to support them than ever before. Even though our techniques have become more refined and sophisticated, the information and communications process involved in decision-making among the voters will continue to be more complex.

MORE TICKET-SPLITTING, NOT LESS

For several reasons, the 1970's will see more ticket-splitting, not less. People under thirty years of age are oriented to audio-visual media, principally television, because they are the first generation to grow up in the environment of this media. They view television as a more authoritative news source than print media. They learn most about politics from television.

Young voters coming into the electorate during the 1970's do not strongly identify with either political party. With the ratification of the eighteen-year-old vote we will see more young voters at a faster rate than ever in our history. Most of these new voters see themselves as independents rather than Democrats or Republicans. They will operationalize this identification by splitting their ballots between the candidates of both parties, with very little loyalty to either party.

DIMINISHING PARTY IMPORTANCE

Heavier and more diversified media use for information on politics will continue to diminish the role of political parties and other variables traditionally associated with the explanation of voting behavior. Party organization leaders will be more and more reduced to organizational roles, leaving the discussion of issues and positions to candidates and officeholders.

Yet the data on ticket-splitters shows that a fundamental realignment of the two political parties is *not* occurring, as Kevin Phillips has argued.[4] We see a stabilizing of the two parties, with no large national shifts occurring from one to the other. The hardcore support of both parties will probably continue to be made up of generally the same kinds of voters. Massive efforts by party leaders to build the two political parties by increasing the number of members or identifiers will probably be met with disappointment and failure.

PREDICTION MORE DIFFICULT

Even though the number of private and public polls about politics and government will increase, it will become more difficult to predict voting behavior and election outcomes. If ticket-splitters continue what they did in 1970 (holding off on their decisions on candidates until late in the campaign), it will make precise predictions hazardous. We do not see the building of simulation models, such as the one constructed by the Simulmatics Corporation for the 1960 Kennedy campaign, as a way to make voter behavior predictions more precise.[5] They consume too much time and money in their construction and are not "dynamic" enough to explain complex human behavioral relationships. With accurate polling instruments, it is possible to get more useful information by telephone than can be gotten by a voter simulation.

TICKET-SPLITTERS AND THE MEDIA

Fundamental changes occurred in the way voters used the media during the 1960's. Most voters today rely on television and radio, rather than newspapers, to report the news. As we have noted, ticket-splitters make up their minds mainly on the basis of the information they get

[4] *The Emerging Republican Majority* (New Rochelle, N.Y.: Arlington House, 1969).

[5] See *Candidates, Issues and Strategies*, by Pool, Popkin, and Abelson (Cambridge: Massachusetts Institute of Technology Press, 1965).

from television newscasts, documentaries, and specials. And television will become increasingly important in political decision-making in the future because of the reliance of young people on it and because of the proliferation of channels in cable television. While in the past the function of *interpreting* (as opposed to reporting) the news has been left to the large daily newspapers, this role, too, will be increasingly played by television. Television will be expected to do more interpretation and in-depth coverage of public affairs.

TICKET-SPLITTERS AND ADVERTISING

Political advertising in the 1970's will look less like traditional advertising (i.e., trying to "sell" candidates) and will be more issue and problem oriented. This will come about because political media producers—taking clues from studies like this one—will structure their commercials using television newscast formats, mini-documentaries, and confrontation situations in simulated press conferences, debates, and talk shows.

In these paid time segments, candidates will have to demonstrate their understanding of public problems and their ability to handle them. Equally important, the candidates of the 1970's will have to demonstrate competence in the handling of media, particularly television.

"PUBLIC" SURVEYS

It has become quite clear that the public polls (Gallup and Harris), with small surveys aimed for newspaper markets, do not explain in depth what is occurring in the electorate. It is also clear that political scientists and other academics who study and try to explain voting behavior do not have the financial resources necessary to do the work. The last definitive "text" on American voting behavior, *The American Voter*, was written about attitudes and voting behavior in the 1950's.

The American people need to understand better the democratic decision-making process. The 1960's witnessed a leveling off of participation in elections at the same time more people became eligible to vote.[6] During this time they received more information about politics and government than ever before. Most of us believed that if citizens knew more about government, their interest in it would increase, and therefore, so would their participation. Now we find that the more Americans know about their government and its political leaders, the more alienated they become. Government can best build support for itself and related political processes by knowing and doing what the electorate wants. This, of course, is how representative government is supposed to perform.

"POLITICAL INDICATORS"

The national government maintains an elaborate information system designed to measure economic performance. "Economic indicators" such as the Consumer Price Index, the Unemployment Survey, the Wholesale & Retail Trade Index, and Housing Starts, all keep track of the economy and allow for some rational planning and control of it.

Alvin Toffler, in his book *Future Shock*, argues that we need a set of comparable " 'social indicators' to tell us whether the society, as distinct from the economy, is also healthy."[7] We agree but would take this proposal one step further. It is critical that there be "political indicators" as well. All of us—not just those who hold public office—need to know how all Americans feel about contemporary problems. Precise measurements of the way voters see policy alternatives to solve these public problems are needed. We need to know how Americans view the political process, and we need to know the changes they would like to see in our political institutions. We need to know if Americans believe they are achieving their personal and societal goals and where they believe this country should head in the future.

When we do not know these things, it becomes difficult,

[6] See *Voter Participation & Registration*, Current Population Reports, Bureau of the Census (1964-1970 post-election turnout studies).

[7] Chapter 20, "The Strategy of Social Futurism" (New York: Random House, 1970).

as Toffler observed, to "connect up national or local policies with appropriate long term social goals."[8] With social and political indicators based on careful measurements, we could provide the kind of information system which would make our nation understand and therefore govern itself better.

Part of the national political malaise and distrust of government—particularly among ticket-splitters—stems from the fact that too often there is a disparity between reality and what is perceived as reality in Washington, D.C., and the state capitals. Today's media are instantaneous communications networks capable of providing information about politics and government with unbelievable speed. It is now possible to create understanding and build attitudes on complex problems overnight, as in the case of the 1971 incursions into Laos and Cambodia. It is possible not only to create attitudes on problems, but to measure them almost instantaneously. The machinery for these measurements already exists. Survey instruments like the one the Bureau of the Census uses to measure economic indicators (the current population survey of 50,000 households across the country each month) could be used to measure social and political indicators as well. Expanding to a similar governmental survey instrument that would include questions on national public issues (not candidates or officeholders) could be done at a relatively small cost. An advisory commission to the Federal agency that would sponsor such a periodic survey, with representatives of the White House, Congress, the national press, and our national universities, could act as advisors on question-content, presentation, and data analysis. Technologically, we are even approaching the time when governments could conduct referenda on public affairs via television or telephones.

CONCLUSION

Our study of the ticket-splitter concludes on the same note struck by V. O. Key in *The Responsible Electorate*,

---

[8] Alvin Toffler, *Future Shock*, p. 403.

namely "that voters are not fools."[9] This includes the ticket-splitters. In fact, American ticket-splitters know just as much about American politics and government and are just as concerned about public problems as behavioral Republicans and Democrats. Moreover, in rating the candidates and officeholders on the basis of the issues and how they handle them, the ticket-splitters make rational decisions. They split their tickets among the two major political parties since all the candidates of one party do not represent what they think are the best alternatives. These are the most discriminating voters in our democratic system and offer the best hope for the revitalization of our unique American democracy. They will be the third force in the politics of the 1970's—they are the new independent electorate.

[9] *The Responsible Electorate* (New York: Random House, 1966), p. 7.

Appendices

A

A Glossary of Terms Describing Independent Voting

1. Ticket-splitter: An involved voter who rationally splits his ballot from President to state legislative races in a single election and tends to split his vote in successive elections. He is basically a Republican or Democrat who splits off occasionally to vote for a candidate of another party. We have had two types of splitters in mind—the Presidential ticket-splitter and the gubernatorial ticket-splitter. The Presidential splitter votes for a President of one party and a governor of another, while a gubernatorial splitter votes for a governor of one party and a candidate for a lower statewide office (e.g., state treasurer or attorney general) from another.

2. Switch Voter: Generally a person who votes for one party in one election, and then for a different party in a later election, though he could also be a person who splits his ballot in a single election. He is considered to be less politically involved than the ticket-splitter, and he tends to evaluate the party performances over a longer span of time.

3. Swing Voters: Persons who traditionally are thought to hold the "balance of power" in any election. These voters are actually ticket-splitters who are located disproportionately in certain geographic areas of a district or a state, and can be identified using aggregate election statistics.

4. Independents: Persons who are truly independent in their political thinking (in a normative sense) and will refuse to be classified into either of the two major parties. However, their true independence in actual voting situations is today confused, as many persons use the independent label as only a political screen. Traditionally, the independent is seen as less politically involved than regular party members, and having only a very marginal effect on the election process.

5. Undecideds: Persons who cannot make up their minds as to their candidate preferences and may not even vote because of this dilemma. These people may include Republican or Democratic identifiers, but are primarily composed of ticket-splitters.

6. Floating Voter: Generally a British label for voters who change their party preferences between elections. They are consistently straight-ticket voters, but with either party, over many elections.

7. Party Shifters: Persons who change their minds during a single election. These people make a pre-election choice to vote for one candidate but then shift over to the opposite candidate near the end of the campaign. These voters tend to be moved especially by issues and the candidates' personalities.

B

Past Efforts to Classify Ticket-splitters

★The Survey Research Center at the University of Michigan tried to create a typology of voters that would include split-ticket voters.[1] Their single effort divided ballot-splitters into five categories:

(1) Those who vote a straight ticket except for President.

(2) Those who vote a straight ticket except for Congressman or senator.

(3) Those who vote a straight ticket at the national level (President, senator, and Congressman), but a straight ticket for the opposite party at the state and local level.

(4) Those who vote a straight ticket at the national level but split at the state and local level.

(5) Those who split their ticket at both the national and local levels.

★Another typology of independence in voting was established by Samuel Eldersveld a few years earlier and was based on a national sample from the 1948 elections. His study produced this typology:

(a) split-ticket voters
(b) those who transfer allegiance over time
(c) voters with no crystallized party predispositions
(d) those who waver in making a voting decision
(e) minor-party supporters.

[1] Angus Campbell and Warren Miller, "The Motivational Basis of Straight and Split-Ticket Voting," *American Political Science Review*, June 1957.

Eldersveld further subclassified the split-ticket voter into party shifters of high frequency and party shifters who split the ballot only occasionally.[2]

★In his little volume on "floating voters," or voters who change their party preference between elections (as distinct from those who shift during a single election, sometimes subclassified as "early changers," "waverers," and "late changers"), H. Daudt defines three kinds:

(1) *Party Changers*—Those who vote for Party A at one election and for Party B at the next.

(2) *Crystallizers*—Those who abstain at one election and vote for one or other of the parties at the next.

(3) *Disintegrators*—Those who have voted for one of the parties at one election but abstain from voting on the next occasion.[3]

★Five years after Daudt's book was published, V. O. Key, Jr., also became concerned about voting in successive elections and the effects of switch-party voting.[4] He broadly classified voters as "standpatters," those who vote for the candidate of the same party in successive elections, "switchers," and the "new voters." Key demonstrated that the party shifters (i.e., ticket-splitters) move from party to party "in a manner broadly consistent with their policy preferences," and that switchers were far more numerous (and rational) than is commonly supposed.

C

Ticket-splitting Options

Current political science literature views ticket-splitting as behavior that is confined to Presidential and Congressional contests. However, a number of other combinations are evident: President and governor, governor and U. S. Senator, governor and some other statewide administrative posts (attorney general, secretary of state, and the like), governor and state legislators, and so forth. Illustrated below are some of the possible options for a split-ticket ballot:

[2] "The Independent Vote: Measurement, Characteristics, and Implications for Party Strategy," *American Political Science Review*, September 1952.

[3] *Floating Voters and the Floating Vote* (Leiden, Holland: H. E. Stenfert, Kroese N. V., 1961).

[4] *The Responsible Electorate* (New York: Random House, 1966).

TABLE 27

Six Options for a Split-Ticket Ballot

	Rep.	Dem.	Rep.	Dem.	Rep.	Dem.
Pres.	R			D	R	
Sen.		D	R			D
Cong.	R			D		D
Gov.		D	R		R	
Total:	2R	2D	2R	2D	2R	2D

	Rep.	Dem.	Rep.	Dem.	Rep.	Dem.
Pres.		D	R			D
Sen.	R		R			D
Cong.	R			D	R	
Gov.		D		D	R	
Total:	2R	2D	2R	2D	2R	2D

Other options include straight-ticket voting, the traditional Presidential splitting in national elections, and deviate splitting when third-party candidates are offered to the voters:

TABLE 28

	Rep.	Dem.		Rep.	Dem.
Pres.	R				D
Sen.	R				D
Cong.	R				D
Gov.	R				D
	4R	0		0	4D

Traditional Presidential Splitter (2 Options)

	Rep.	Dem.		Rep.	Dem.
Pres.	R				D
Sen.		D		R	
Cong.		D		R	
Gov.		D		R	
	1R(P)	3D		3R	1D(P)

Deviant Ticket-Splitting (e.g., Wallace in 1968)

	Rep.	Dem.	A.I.	Rep.	Dem.	A.I.
Pres.			W			W
Sen.		D		R		
Cong.		D		R		
Gov.		D		R		
		3D	W	3R		W

While the above broad combinations and incidences of ticket-splitting are the ones most frequently observed in political science literature, a person could, of course, split his ticket completely from top to bottom, instead of in such broad categories. If he did, it would probably reflect the ultimate in political sophistication or acute schizophrenia.

The voter has several options that he must consider when evaluating the election system and his possible entry into it:

(1) Non-vote
(2) Straight Democratic vote
(3) Straight Republican vote
(4) Straight minor party vote
(5) Split ballot between major-party candidates.

The voter must exercise one of these options every time he decides to cast his ballot (whether a complete or incomplete one) in any general election. Thus, a voter must make actually *three* broad decisions in every election: whether to vote at all, whether he will vote a straight or split-ticket, and which candidates or party will be his choice or choices. The voter has twenty-five options to consider before he makes the single candidate choice:

TABLE 29
VOTE OPTIONS THROUGH TIME

1. From non-voting	to		straight Republican
2. From non-voting	to		straight Democratic
3. From non-voting	to		straight minor party
4. From non-voting	to		split ticket
5. From straight Republican		to	non-voting
6. From straight Republican		to	straight Democratic
7. From straight Republican		to	straight minor party
8. From straight Republican		to	split ticket
9. From straight Democratic		to	non-voting
10. From straight Democratic		to	straight Republican
11. From straight Democratic		to	straight minor party
12. From straight Democratic		to	split ticket
13. From minor party	to		non-voting
14. From minor party	to		straight Republican
15. From minor party	to		straight Democratic
16. From minor party	to		split ticket
17. From split ticket	to		non-voting
18. From split ticket	to		straight Republican
19. From split ticket	to		straight Democratic
20. From split ticket	to		straight minor party
21. Continue non-voting			
22. Continue straight Republican			
23. Continue straight Democratic			
24. Continue minor party			
25. Continue split ticket			

D

A Paradigm of Voting in State "X"

To understand how split-ticket voters do control the outcome of competitive elections, examine the following theoretical paradigm. Assume that we conduct a survey in state X which reveals that the state's voters consider themselves as follows: [5]

SELF-PERCEPTION

Democrats	43.3%
Republicans	28.9
Independents	26.6
Don't know	1.2
	100.0

State X appears to be a predominantly Democratic state with a 14.4% edge over Republicans. Assume that there are one million voters in state X and that voter turnout will be 100% except for the "don't knows." There will be 433,000 Democrats, 289,000 Republicans, and 266,000 self-classified independents. Neither party has the required 500,000 votes to win by itself. The Republican disadvantage is obvious.

In a post-election survey, however, we find that the voting patterns were exceedingly complex: [6]

Self-Classified Definition	Actual Behavioral Recall (Ranked)	
Republicans	Voted straight Republican	77.2%
	Voted split ballots	21.7
	Voted straight Democratic	1.1

[5] Determined by asking the respondents "Do you consider yourself a Democrat or a Republican, or what?"

[6] Determined by asking respondents how they voted for President, for state governor, for state treasurer (bedrock vote), etc.

(Continued)

Self-Classified Definition	Actual Behavioral Recall (Ranked)	
Democrats	Voted straight Democratic	61.4%
	Voted split ballots	34.0
	Voted straight Republican	4.6
Independents	Voted split ballots	61.9%
	Voted straight Republican	27.1
	Voted straight Democratic	11.0

The following diagram illustrates the cross directions of the perceptual and behavioral approaches in looking at election outcomes:

TICKET SPLITTING

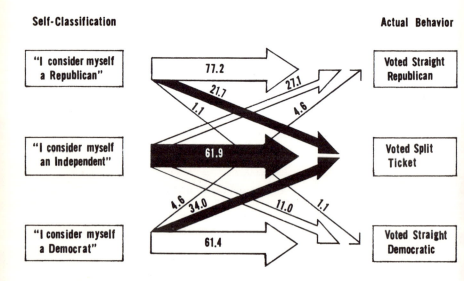

When we calculate the actual vote strength in the model state (with a 98.8% turnout of the one million voters) the coalitions or vote alignments become clear:

Republican Party

223,108	Republicans who voted straight Republican ticket
72,086	Independents who voted straight Republican ticket
19,918	Democrats who voted straight Republican ticket
total: 315,112	

Democratic Party

265,862	Democrats who voted straight Democratic ticket
29,260	Independents who voted straight Democratic ticket
3,179	Republicans who voted straight Democratic ticket
total: 298,301	

Ticket-Splitters

164,654	Independents who voted a split ticket
147,220	Democrats who voted a split ticket
62,713	Republicans who voted a split ticket
total: 374,587	

Despite the survey results showing that only 28.9% of the total eligible voters considered themselves Republicans, the Republican candidate in our model state would actually have more votes than the Democratic candidate if the ticket-splitters were excluded (315,112 to 298,301). However, there were nearly 375,000 ticket-splitters who clearly held the balance of power in this election.

The ticket-splitters cast more votes than either the Republicans or the Democrats. (Of the total vote, 32.1% of all voters cast straight Republican ballots, 30% straight Democratic ballots, and 38% split-ticket ballots.)

If a ticket-splitter strategy were employed that merely halved the ticket-splitter vote, the Republican candidate would still win a very tight race:

Republican Candidate		Democratic Candidate	
315,112	Straight Republican Voters	298,301	Straight Democratic Voters
187,293	Ticket-splitters	187,293	Ticket-splitters
502,405	(50.1%)	485,594	(49.9%)

As another possibility within this example, assume that the Republican candidate directed his campaign to both Republicans and ticket-splitters and was successful in winning two-thirds of all voters who cast split ballots (66% of 374,587 split-ticket votes). The Republican candidate would then win state X, nominally a Democratic state, in a landslide:

Republican Candidate		Democratic Candidate	
315,112	Straight Republican Voters	298,301	Straight Democratic Voters
250,973	Ticket-splitters	123,614	Ticket-splitters
566,085	(57.1%)	421,915	(42.9%)

This overall model suggests, then, that Republican candidates who can capture voters who exhibit high propensities to split their ballots may have not only a fifty-fifty chance for election victory, but a chance for an actual landslide even though their party is a minority party. These results occur today in many states, despite the way the voters perceive themselves.

E

A Ticket-splitting Campaign Formula

How would a Republican in a predominantly Democratic state initiate a strategy that would be successful? First of all, he would calculate a minimum-victory formula that would concentrate on Republicans and ticket-splitters. Secondly, he would view the relative size of the Republican core vote as absolutely critical—the loss of a few percentage points in Republican support would be catastrophic to the strategy. It must be kept in mind that when people discuss Republican strength on the basis of either polling data or voting data, they face the natural and dangerous tendency to use the highest winning Republican race in some past election and to base their thinking on a percentage of, say, 58% or 60%. Rather, estimates *must* be based on the gross concept developed from polling data (e.g., as in the model state discussed previously) and *not* just from the net concept based on net aggregate voting data.

For example, assume that there are several states with the core Republican vote at the following:

25%	State X
30%	State Y
40%	State Z

What happens if we assume that a Republican candidate will get 90% of this vote, but varying amounts of the ticket-splitter vote? Looking at Table 30, assume that the size of the total ticket-splitter vote (in our model it was 38%) can vary from 20% to 40%, as registered down the left-hand side of the table, and note the percentage of that vote horizontally which will give the net percent of the vote from the ticket-splitter total vote.

TABLE 30

NET VOTE OF TICKET-SPLITTER

		Amount of Ticket-Splitter Vote Voting Republican			
	%	50%	60%	75%	90%
Size of Ticket-	20	10.0	12.0	15.0	18.0
Splitter in total	30	15.0	18.0	22.5	27.0
Voting population	40	20.0	24.0	30.0	36.0

Assuming then that a Republican candidate has a Republican core vote of 25% and he wins 90% of it, this means he starts with 25% x .9, which equals 22.4% of the total vote. Then let's assume that of the total voting population 30% are ticket-splitters. By looking at Table 30 we then have the following results:

	Ticket-Splitter Strategy	Total Vote % before Democrat cross-overs
Plan A.	If we take 50% of ticket-splitters, then 22.4 + 15.0 . . . equals	37.4
Plan B.	If we take 60% of ticket-splitters, then 22.4 + 18.0 . . . equals	40.4
Plan C.	If we take 75% of ticket-splitters, then 22.4 + 22.5 . . . equals	44.9

Thus, one can see that Plan C and perhaps Plan B have the only chance to win—and these only if enough Democratic partisans cross over to the Republican side (Plan B requires an additional 9.7% Democratic vote while Plan C requires a 5.2% cross-over). The Republican candidate strategy in state X can be summarized as follows: 90% of total Republican identifiers, plus 75% of the ticket-splitter vote, and 12% of Democratic identifiers equals victory. The mathematical equation looks like this:

Republican Formula = .90R + .75 TS + .12D

	if R = Republican total vote (25%)
For State X	if TS = Ticket-splitter vote (30%)
	if D = Democratic vote (45%)
	For R .90 x 25 = 22.4
	For TS .75 x 30 = 22.5
	For D .12 x 45 = 5.4
	Total vote: 50.3

Assume, in one more example, that the Republican core strength is somewhat higher and on a par with the Democrats, as in state Z. If we still assume that the Republican candidate must hold at least 90% of his party identifiers, that would be 40% x .9, which equals 36.0%. With a stronger base to work from, the Republican candidate can be slightly more flexible in the rest of his strategy.

Calculating a ticket-splitter goal of 60% and only 10% of the Democrats, we have the following equation:

Republican Formula = .90R + .60TS + .10D

	For R .90 x 40 = 36.0
For State Z	For TS .60 x 20 = 12.0
	For D .10 x 40 = 4.0
	Total vote: 52.0

In conclusion, a typical strategy for a Republican Presidential or statewide candidate is a complex one. Republican candidates cannot rely on identifying only the Republicans, independents and Democrats because, as in our model state, this self-perceived approach does not represent actual voting behavior. In order to win, Republicans must identify from past election data the voters who consistently split their ballot. The Republican Party's increased ability to win individual state elections during the past "Democratic decade" is most likely due to its appeal to the candidate and issue perceptions of the ticket-splitters, and to the statistical techniques which utilize survey and voting data to identify these splitters.[7]

F

Census Bureau Estimates on Young Voters in 1972

Approximately 140 million men and women will be old enough to vote in the November 1972 Presidential election, according to new estimates from the Bureau of the Census, U. S. Department of Commerce. Of this number, some 25 million young people under the age of twenty-five will be eligible to vote for President for the first time—about the same as the total number who voted for both Warren G. Harding and James M. Cox in the 1920 election (25,299,553).

The exceptionally large number of new voters is the result of the Voting Rights Act Amendment of 1970, which lowered the voting age in national elections to eighteen in all states after January 1, 1971. This means that all people between the ages of eighteen and twenty-four in November 1972 will be potential first-time voters. By lowering the age requirement, some 11 million persons will be enfranchised who would not have been eligible to vote under the previous laws. A constitutional amendment, passed by Congress and ratified by three-fourths of the state legislatures, has extended the eighteen-year-old vote to include state and local elections.

California and New York are expected to have the greatest number of new voters in 1972—more than 2 million each. Texas, Pennsylvania, Ohio, Illinois, and Michigan will each have more than one million potential new voters.

In the nation as a whole, persons under twenty-five will make up an estimated 18% of the total electorate for the 1972 Presidential election. Young people will exert the greatest relative influence in South Carolina and Utah (23%). In Georgia and Kentucky, where eighteen- to twenty-year-olds are already voting, about 11% of the voting-age population will be newly enfranchised.

The extent to which these potential young voters will affect

[7] See Chapter V for actual campaign applications of the ticket-splitter concept.

voting patterns in America is not known. In the Presidential election of 1968, about half of the population in the twenty-one to twenty-four age group reported themselves as having voted. For the rest of the population, 68% said they went to the polls. The information is based on the November 1968 Current Population Survey conducted by the Bureau of the Census one week after the election.

It should be noted that the 1972 voting-age population will include many persons who are old enough to vote but cannot do so for many reasons. They may, for example, be aliens or persons committed to mental hospitals and other institutions.

The attached table gives a breakdown by region and individual states on the estimated number of new voters, both under the old law and the Voting Rights Act Amendment of 1970.

ESTIMATES OF THE TOTAL RESIDENT POPULATION OF VOTING AGE, NOVEMBER 1972

(Numbers in Thousands)

Region, Division, and State	Population of Voting Age (18 yrs. & over)	NEW VOTERS		
		Total	Population Reaching Voting Age Since 1968 Under Old Law[8]	Population Enfranchised Due to Lowering Voting Age to 18
United States, Total	139,563	25,125	13,966	11,159
Regions				
Northeastern States	34,075	5,723	3,118	2,605
North Central States	38,038	7,048	3,810	3,238
The South	43,077	7,832	4,553	3,279
The West	24,372	4,523	2,485	2,038
Northeast				
New England	8,208	1,483	808	675
Middle Atlantic	25,867	4,241	2,311	1,930
North Central				
East North Central	27,038	4,988	2,697	2,291
West North Central	11,000	2,060	1,113	947

[8] Persons reaching age 21 except Hawaii (reaching age 20), Alaska (reaching age 19), and Georgia and Kentucky (reaching age 18).

ESTIMATES OF THE TOTAL RESIDENT POPULATION (Continued)

Region, Division, and State	Population of Voting Age (18 yrs. & over)	NEW VOTERS		
		Total	Population Reaching Voting Age Since 1968 Under Old Law	Population Enfran- chised Due to Lower- ing Voting Age to 18
South				
South Atlantic	21,434	3,787	2,234	1,553
East South Central	8,589	1,503	936	567
West South Central	13,054	2,543	1,384	1,159
West				
Mountain	5,559	1,103	601	502
Pacific	18,813	3,420	1,884	1,536
New England				
Maine	662	122	67	55
New Hampshire	511	95	51	44
Vermont	301	64	34	30
Massachusetts	3,947	725	395	330
Rhode Island	671	135	75	60
Connecticut	2,117	343	187	156
Middle Atlantic				
New York	12,714	2,101	1,147	954
New Jersey	5,018	769	419	350
Pennsylvania	8,136	1,371	745	626
East North Central				
Ohio	7,165	1,313	713	600
Indiana	3,487	662	359	303
Illinois	7,563	1,321	716	605
Michigan	5,875	1,127	607	520
Wisconsin	2,948	565	302	263
West North Central				
Minnesota	2,523	478	257	221
Iowa	1,887	347	187	160
Missouri	3,222	569	308	261
North Dakota	398	83	45	38

ESTIMATES OF THE TOTAL RESIDENT POPULATION (Continued)

Region, Division, and State	Population of Voting Age (18 yrs. & over)	NEW VOTERS		
		Total	Population Reaching Voting Age Since 1968 Under Old Law	Population Enfran-chised Due to Lower-ing Voting Age to 18
South Dakota	430	88	47	41
Nebraska	1,002	191	103	88
Kansas	1,539	304	166	138
South Atlantic				
Delaware	372	68	37	31
Maryland	2,715	478	262	216
District of Columbia	534	111	63	48
Virginia	3,232	645	359	286
West Virginia	1,175	217	118	99
North Carolina	3,493	750	409	341
South Carolina	1,715	391	213	178
Georgia	3,111	354	354	—[9]
Florida	5,088	773	419	354
East South Central				
Kentucky	2,177	254	254	—[9]
Tennessee	2,710	511	279	232
Alabama	2,291	440	241	199
Mississippi	1,412	297	161	136
West South Central				
Arkansas	1,318	230	126	104
Louisiana	2,356	497	267	230
Oklahoma	1,791	325	178	147
Texas	7,589	1,490	812	678
Mountain				
Montana	452	84	46	38
Idaho	467	90	48	42
Wyoming	217	40	22	18
Colorado	1,532	319	174	145
New Mexico	633	129	71	58
Arizona	1,227	232	125	107

[9] Population already enfranchised.

ESTIMATES OF THE TOTAL RESIDENT POPULATION (Continued)

Region, Division, and State	Population of Voting Age (18 yrs. & over)	NEW VOTERS		
		Total	Population Reaching Voting Age Since 1968 Under Old Law	Population Enfranchised Due to Lowering Voting Age to 18
Utah	674	154	84	70
Nevada	356	54	30	24
Pacific				
Washington	2,381	460	249	211
Oregon	1,473	259	140	119
California	14,237	2,580	1,411	1,169
Alaska	193	29	23	6
Hawaii	528	91	60	31

G

Census Bureau Profile of the Average American Family in 1970

The average American family is composed of a husband, wife, and two children in their late teens, according to data from the Bureau of the Census. This typical family is slightly smaller than in the past, and there are some differences in ages. Compared with, say, 1950, today's family has fewer children under five years of age but more over sixteen. The reason for this is the declining birth rate in recent years.

Parents are a bit older, too. The average husband and father is just short of his forty-fifth birthday and his wife a little short of her forty-second. A generation ago they both were a year or so younger.

As a result of the increased emphasis on education, the parents of today's children have had about three years more schooling than their parents had. The average number of years of schooling in 1950 was about nine years—today it is twelve years. In other words, most parents of young children today have about the equivalent of a high school education.

Incomes are higher today than they were two decades ago. In 1970, the median family income was $9,870, as compared with $3,300 in 1950. But prices are higher, too. Nevertheless, the typical family has more "real" income now than it had in 1950. By giving the 1970 dollar the same purchasing power as the 1950 dollar had, comparisons in "real" terms can be made. On that basis, the typical 1970 family had an income of $6,100, almost twice as much as the $3,300 income of the typical family in 1950.

The head of the family earns more than twice as much as a generation ago, and the income brought in by his wife or other members of the family is likely to be greater because more wives and other family members are working today than was the case in 1950. The husband works the full year—fifty weeks with a two-week paid vacation on the average. He most likely is employed in a private industry or business as a craftsman, foreman, or operative. He works in an urban area and drives to and from work in the family's one car, or he may belong to a car pool.

Today's typical family is likely to live in a metropolitan area, probably in a suburb. Nearly 70% of the U.S. population lives in metropolitan areas, and over half of the metropolitan population lives in areas outside the central cities.

The family's house is better and larger than a generation ago. It has five rooms instead of four. It is about twenty-five years old and is almost sure to have complete kitchen and bathroom facilities, hot piped water, and central heating. The wife most likely has a clothes washing machine, but probably not a clothes dryer, dishwasher, or home freezer. The family has at least one television set, a radio, and a telephone, but is not likely to have air conditioning.

The 1970 family is likely to own its home, with a mortgage. The average home today is valued at $17,000, a 43% increase over the average home value noted ten years ago in the 1960 census. This is the median value of one-family, non-farm, owner-occupied homes. The family spends about $265 a year on upkeep and improvements on the house.

H

The Distribution of Party Identification in the United States, 1952-1970

Question: "Generally speaking, do you usually think of yourself as a Republican, a Democrat, an Independent, or what? (IF REPUBLICAN OR DEMOCRAT) Would you call yourself a strong (R) (D) or a not very strong (R) (D)? (IF INDEPENDENT) Do you think of yourself as closer to the Republican or Democratic Party?"

	Oct. 1952	Oct. 1954	Oct. 1956	Oct. 1958	Oct. 1960	Nov. 1962	Oct. 1964	Nov. 1966	Nov. 1968	Nov. 1970
Democrat										
Strong	22%	22%	21%	23%	21%	23%	26%	18%	20%	20%
Weak	25	25	23	24	25	23	25	27	25	23
Independent										
Democrat	10	9	7	7	8	8	9	9	10	10
Independent	5	7	9	8	8	8	8	12	11	13
Republican	7	6	8	4	7	6	6	7	9	8
Republican										
Weak	14	14	14	16	13	16	13	15	14	15
Strong	13	13	15	13	14	12	11	10	10	10
Apolitical, Don't know	4	4	3	5	4	4	2	2	1	1
Total	100%	100%	100%	100%	100%	100%	100%	100%	100%	100%
Number of Cases	1614	1139	1772	1269	3021	1289	1571	1291	1553	1802

Center for Political Studies
The University of Michigan

November, 1970

I

The Heavyweight Voter Areas for the
Political Contests of the 1970's

The following is a list by rank of the fifty most populous urbanized areas in the United States, based on the results of the 1970 Decennial Census (an urbanized area consists of a city of 50,000 persons or more, plus the densely built-up adjoining area—suburbs—whether incorporated or not):

Rank	Urbanized Area	Urbanized 1970 Population
1	New York, N.Y.-Northeastern New Jersey	16,206,841
2	Los Angeles-Long Beach, Calif.	8,351,266
3	Chicago, Ill.-Northwestern Indiana	6,714,578
4	Philadelphia, Pa.-N.J.	4,021,066
5	Detroit, Mich.	3,970,584
6	San Francisco-Oakland, Calif.	2,987,850
7	Boston, Mass.	2,652,575
8	Washington, D.C.-Md.-Va.	2,481,489
9	Cleveland, Ohio	1,959,880
10	St. Louis, Mo.-Ill.	1,882,944
11	Pittsburgh, Pa.	1,846,042
12	Minneapolis-St. Paul, Minn.	1,704,423
13	Houston, Texas	1,677,863
14	Baltimore, Md.	1,579,781
15	Dallas, Texas	1,338,684
16	Milwaukee, Wis.	1,252,457
17	Seattle-Everett, Wash.	1,238,107
18	Miami, Fla.	1,219,661
19	San Diego, Calif.	1,198,323
20	Atlanta, Ga.	1,172,778
21	Cincinnati, Ohio-Ky.	1,110,514
22	Kansas City, Mo.-Kans.	1,101,787
23	Buffalo, N.Y.	1,086,594

(Continued)

Rank	Urbanized Area	Urbanized 1970 Population
24	Denver, Colo.	1,047,311
25	San Jose, Calif.	1,025,273
26	New Orleans, La.	961,728
27	Phoenix, Ariz.	863,357
28	Portland, Ore.-Wash.	824,926
29	Indianapolis, Ind.	820,259
30	Providence-Pawtucket-Warwick, R.I.-Mass.	795,311
31	Columbus, Ohio	790,019
32	San Antonio, Texas	772,513
33	Louisville, Ky.-Ind.	739,396
34	Dayton, Ohio	685,942
35	Fort Worth, Texas	676,944
36	Norfolk-Portsmouth, Va.	668,259
37	Memphis, Tenn.-Miss.	663,976
38	Sacramento, Calif.	633,732
39	Fort Lauderdale-Hollywood, Fla.	613,797
40	Rochester, N.Y.	601,361
41	San Bernardino-Riverside, Calif.	583,597
42	Oklahoma City, Okla.	579,788
43	Birmingham, Ala.	558,099
44	Akron, Ohio	542,775
45	Jacksonville, Fla.	529,585
46	Springfield-Chicopee-Holyoke, Mass.-Conn.	514,308
47	St. Petersburg, Fla.	495,159
48	Omaha, Nebr.-Iowa	491,776
49	Toledo, Ohio-Mich.	487,789
50	Albany-Schenectady-Troy, N.Y.	486,525
	Total	87,209,592

J

Estimates of the Total Resident Population of Voting Age by Age Groupings in 1972

Region, Division, and State	POPULATION OF VOTING AGE (000's)	18-20 Number (000's)	18-20 Percent %	21-24 Number (000's)	21-24 Percent %
United States, Total	139,563	11,660	100.0	13,765	100.0
Regions					
Northeastern States	34,075	2,605	22.3	3,115	22.6
North Central States	38,038	3,238	27.8	3,649	26.5
The South	43,077	3,754	32.2	4,391	31.9
The West	24,372	2,066	17.7	2,611	19.0
Northeast					
New England	8,208	675	5.8	812	5.9
Middle Atlantic	25,867	1,930	16.5	2,303	16.7
North Central					
East North Central	27,038	2,291	19.7	2,625	19.1
West North Central	11,000	947	8.1	1,023	7.4
South					
South Atlantic	21,434	1,831	15.7	2,214	16.1
East South Central	8,589	764	6.6	835	6.1
West South Central	13,054	1,159	9.9	1,341	9.7
West					
Mountain	5,559	502	4.3	593	4.3
Pacific	18,813	1,564	13.4	2,018	14.7
New England					
Maine	662	55	0.5	60	0.4
New Hampshire	511	44	0.4	50	0.4
Vermont	301	30	0.3	30	0.2
Massachusetts	3,947	330	2.8	396	2.9
Rhode Island	671	60	0.5	74	0.5
Connecticut	2,117	156	1.3	201	1.5
Middle Atlantic					
New York	12,714	954	8.2	1,163	8.5
New Jersey	5,018	350	3.0	438	3.2
Pennsylvania	8,136	626	5.4	702	5.1
East North Central					
Ohio	7,165	600	5.2	697	5.1
Indiana	3,487	303	2.6	345	2.5
Illinois	7,563	605	5.2	705	5.1
Michigan	5,875	520	4.5	598	4.3
Wisconsin	2,948	263	2.3	280	2.0
West North Central					
Minnesota	2,523	221	1.9	245	1.8
Iowa	1,887	160	1.4	163	1.2

25-34		35-44		45-64		65+	
Number (000's)	Percent %	Number (000's)	Percent %	Number (000's)	Percent %	Number (000's)	Percent %
27,763	100.0	22,562	100.0	42,913	100.0	20,900	100.0
6,415	23.1	5,515	24.4	11,071	25.8	5,357	25.6
7,500	27.0	6,106	27.1	11,678	27.2	5,868	28.1
8,647	31.1	6,964	30.9	12,908	30.1	6,415	30.7
5,201	18.7	3,976	17.6	7,256	16.9	3,260	15.6
1,558	5.6	1,282	5.7	2,581	6.0	1,301	6.2
4,857	17.5	4,233	18.8	8,489	19.8	4,056	19.4
5,429	19.6	4,418	19.6	8,368	19.5	3,906	18.7
2,071	7.5	1,689	7.5	3,311	7.7	1,961	9.4
4,325	15.6	3,461	15.3	6,451	15.0	3,153	15.1
1,690	6.1	1,372	6.1	2,604	6.1	1,324	6.3
2,633	9.5	2,131	9.4	3,853	9.0	1,938	9.3
1,171	4.2	921	4.1	1,633	3.8	737	3.5
4,030	14.5	3,055	13.5	5,622	13.1	2,523	12.1
118	0.4	106	0.5	206	0.5	116	0.6
102	0.4	81	0.4	153	0.4	81	0.4
60	0.2	46	0.2	87	0.2	48	0.2
738	2.7	605	2.7	1,228	2.9	649	3.1
117	0.4	99	0.4	213	0.5	107	0.5
422	1.5	345	1.5	694	1.6	299	1.4
2,485	9.0	2,075	9.2	4,019	9.4	2,018	9.7
964	3.5	859	3.8	1,677	3.9	730	3.5
1,408	5.1	1,299	5.8	2,793	6.5	1,307	6.3
1,418	5.1	1,185	5.3	2,247	5.2	1,017	4.9
711	2.6	570	2.5	1,055	2.5	503	2.4
1,539	5.5	1,228	5.4	2,368	5.5	1,118	5.4
1,199	4.3	975	4.3	1,805	4.2	778	3.7
562	2.0	460	2.0	893	2.1	489	2.3
515	1.9	386	1.7	735	1.7	421	2.0
344	1.2	286	1.3	578	1.3	355	1.7

Region, Division, and State	POPULATION OF VOTING AGE (000's)	18-20		21-24	
		Number (000's)	Percent %	Number (000's)	Percent %
Missouri	3,222	261	2.2	292	2.1
North Dakota	398	38	0.3	38	0.3
South Dakota	430	41	0.3	37	0.3
Nebraska	1,002	88	0.8	93	0.7
Kansas	1,539	138	1.2	154	1.1
South Atlantic					
Delaware	372	31	0.3	38	0.3
Maryland	2,715	216	1.8	286	2.1
District of Columbia	534	48	0.4	66	0.5
Virginia	3,232	286	2.5	373	2.7
West Virginia	1,175	99	0.8	101	0.7
North Carolina	3,493	341	2.9	379	2.8
South Carolina	1,715	178	1.5	194	1.4
Georgia	3,111	278	2.4	352	2.6
Florida	5,088	354	3.0	426	3.1
East South Central					
Kentucky	2,177	197	1.7	215	1.6
Tennessee	2,710	232	2.0	264	1.9
Alabama	2,291	199	1.7	220	1.6
Mississippi	1,412	136	1.2	136	1.0
West South Central					
Arkansas	1,318	104	0.9	119	0.9
Louisiana	2,356	230	2.0	244	1.8
Oklahoma	1,791	147	1.3	172	1.3
Texas	7,589	678	5.8	805	5.9
Mountain					
Montana	452	38	0.3	41	0.3
Idaho	467	42	0.4	43	0.3
Wyoming	217	18	0.2	20	0.1
Colorado	1,532	145	1.2	178	1.3
New Mexico	633	58	0.5	65	0.5
Arizona	1,227	107	0.9	125	0.9
Utah	674	70	0.6	85	0.6
Nevada	336	24	0.2	36	0.3
Pacific					
Washington	2,381	211	1.8	354	1.8
Oregon	1,473	119	1.0	141	1.0
California	14,237	1,169	10.0	1,523	11.1
Alaska	193	18	0.2	30	0.2
Hawaii	528	47	0.4	71	0.5

(z) = Less than 0.05 percent

25-34		35-44		45-64		65+	
Number (000's)	Percent %	Number (000's)	Percent %	Number (000's)	Percent %	Number (000's)	Percent %
613	2.2	498	2.2	984	2.3	573	2.7
69	0.2	62	0.3	122	0.3	69	0.3
70	0.3	66	0.3	133	0.3	83	0.4
182	0.7	155	0.7	295	0.7	188	0.9
277	1.0	235	1.0	463	1.1	272	1.3
79	0.3	65	0.3	114	0.3	46	0.2
600	2.2	466	2.1	830	1.9	317	1.5
124	0.4	79	0.4	146	0.3	71	0.3
695	2.5	541	2.4	953	2.2	384	1.8
199	0.7	183	0.8	393	0.9	200	1.0
716	2.6	579	2.6	1,037	2.4	441	2.1
356	1.3	280	1.2	506	1.2	201	1.0
688	2.5	512	2.3	896	2.1	386	1.8
868	3.1	756	3.4	1,577	3.7	1,106	5.3
423	1.5	341	1.5	653	1.5	347	1.7
550	2.0	438	1.9	825	1.9	402	1.9
449	1.6	374	1.7	705	1.6	343	1.6
268	1.0	219	1.0	422	1.0	231	1.1
243	0.9	193	0.9	411	1.0	249	1.2
479	1.7	387	1.7	692	1.6	324	1.5
338	1.2	279	1.2	544	1.3	312	1.5
1,573	5.7	1,273	5.6	2,207	5.1	1,054	5.0
87	0.3	72	0.3	144	0.3	69	0.3
92	0.3	72	0.3	147	0.3	70	0.3
43	0.2	37	0.2	68	0.2	31	0.1
334	1.2	257	1.1	425	1.0	194	0.9
134	0.5	114	0.5	186	0.4	76	0.4
249	0.9	197	0.9	369	0.9	181	0.9
146	0.5	107	0.5	184	0.4	82	0.4
86	0.3	65	0.3	110	0.3	34	0.2
495	1.8	365	1.6	726	1.7	330	1.6
292	1.1	220	1.0	464	1.1	237	1.1
3,066	11.0	2,336	10.4	4,243	9.9	1,901	9.1
56	0.2	39	0.2	43	0.1	7	(z)
120	0.4	95	0.4	147	0.3	48	0.2

Source: U.S. CENSUS projections

GAYLORD

PRINTED IN U.S.A.

DATE DUE

9202870